Romero: Martyr for Liberation

Romero: Martyr for Liberation

The last two homilies of

Archbishop Romero of San Salvador

with a theological analysis of his
life and work by

Jon Sobrino SJ

Preface by
Cardinal Basil Hume

Catholic Institute for International Relations

First published in February 1982 by the
Catholic Institute for International Relations,
22 Coleman Fields, London N1 7AF

© Catholic Institute for International Relations 1982

ISBN 0 904393 71 2

'Archbishop Romero: Martyr for Liberation' by Jon Sobrino SJ is
published by kind permission of Orbis Books, Maryknoll, New York.

The chapter by Jon Sobrino was translated by Michael Walsh.

British Library Cataloguing in Publication Data

Romero, Oscar Arnulfo
Romero: martyr for liberation.
1. Theology, Catholic
I. Title II. Sobrino, Jon
230'.2   BX1751.2

Copies available by post from CIIR. Trade distribution to bookshops and
library suppliers by Third World Publications Ltd, 151 Stratford Road,
Birmingham B11 1RD, Tel. 021-773 6572.

Printed by the Russell Press Ltd, Bertrand Russell House,
Nottingham (UK).

Cover design by Jan Brown 01-837 5296
Cover photo by Carlos Reyes

Contents

Preface

El Salvador has suffered a long and cruel agony. The victims are legion. Yet one man stays in the memory as a symbol of Christian devotion and of unusual courage. The assassination of Archbishop Romero in March 1980 shocked the world. He was killed while offering the sacrifice of the mass and while proclaiming the word of God. To the end he was a faithful witness to the Gospel and he sealed that witness with his blood.

We in Britain knew him only from a distance. Many understood his significance only after his murder. Now we have the opportunity to learn more about him through the last two homilies of his life and the study by Fr Sobrino now brought together in this book.

Although our situation and history is vastly different from that of Central America and of El Salvador in particular, the life and witness of Archbishop Romero has importance for us. We do not face comparable injustice and oppression. We do not have to make difficult decisions on the morality of violent resistance to tyranny. Yet Christians everywhere have to live the Gospel in daily life and apply its teaching to the conduct of political, social and economic affairs. Here there can be room for legitimate diversity of views but the effort has to be made, despite contradiction and opposition, to build the city of man within the kingdom of God. Archbishop Romero's life and teaching is a vivid reminder of the price that Christians are sometimes called upon to pay for their vision and their work. We can draw inspiration from his witness and example.

I welcome the publication of this small tribute to the memory of Archbishop Romero. I hope that by this means he will be more widely known. We all need his kind of sanctity and his degree of courage.

Cardinal Basil Hume,
25 January 1982   *Archbishop of Westminster.*

The Church and Human Liberation

Mass readings:
Isaiah 43:16-21
Philippians 3:8-14
John 8:1-11

Introduction

We greet you beloved brothers and sisters visiting El Salvador on an ecumenical mission to study the state of human rights in our country. We are delighted you will share with us in this celebration of God's word and the eucharist.

Concelebrating this mass with me are Franciscan Father Alan McCoy, president of the US Conference of Major Religious Superiors of Men, and Father Juan Macho Merino. Also present is Mr Thomas Quigley, layman of the Latin American section of the Department of Social Development and World Peace of the US Catholic Conference. Present too are: the Rev. William Wipfler of the programme for human rights of the National Council of Churches in the United States; Mrs Betty de Nutte Richardson of the American Friends Service Committee, also in the US; and Mr Ronald Joung of the peace education programme of the same service committee.

We sense in you, our visitors, the sympathy of North America. Because of that sympathy, we understand how the gospel can illuminate various types of societies. One feels solidarity with a church that clearly tries to defend the human rights that are trampled in our country. That solidarity exists because of the respect for human beings our Lord revealed to us.

1

Our thanks to our visitors. May the days you spend with us be extremely beneficial in further strengthening your Christian commitment. In our understanding of other countries, let us see how our efforts are understood and supported by all of those who are illuminated by the light of the gospel.

Greetings also to the listeners of YSAX, our archdiocesan radio station, an instrument of truth and justice. You have long awaited this transmission, and the moment has now arrived, thanks be to God. We know the danger that threatens our poor radio station for being an instrument of truth and justice, but we know the risk must be taken, because an entire people depend on it as they strive to uphold this word of truth and justice.

Greetings also to the listeners of Radio News of the Continent. I am glad to have the collaboration of Radio News. It is carrying our voice from this microphone and through our transmitter to Latin America. Reporter Demetrio Olaziregui is here with us. He told us how a bomb exploded near the studios of the broadcasting station in Costa Rica. Dynamite charges destroyed part of the wall and blew out the windows of a two-storey building. For a short time the station had to go off the air, but it has resumed operations and is performing a marvellous service for us. We are told our homilies will continue to be broadcast since there is demand for them in Venezuela, in Colombia, and from as far away as Brazil. The radio station has received between 300 and 400 letters showing that people hear this broadcast perfectly in Honduras, in Nicaragua, and right here in El Salvador, in many parts of our country.

Lent, preparation for Easter

So we give thanks to God that a message which doesn't claim to be more than a modest reflection of the divine word should find wonderful channels to spread and reach many people. It tells them that in the context of Lent all this is a preparation for our Easter, and that already Easter is indeed a cry of victory. No one can extinguish the life which Christ revived. Not even death or hatred of him and his church will overcome this life. Christ is the victor.

Holy Week is the celebration of redemption: Christ will be glorified in an Easter of unending resurrection. But we have to accompany him in Lent, in a Holy Week that makes his cross, sacrifice and martyrdom real for us. Christ is saying to us: 'Happy are those who are not offended by their cross'.

Lent is, then, a call to celebrate our redemption in the complex relationship of cross and victory. Our people are well equipped for this at the moment since everything around us preaches the cross. But those who have Christian faith and hope know that behind this Calvary of El Salvador is our Easter, our resurrection, and that is the hope of the Christian people.

God's word in Lent reveals his plan to free humanity completely. During these Sundays of Lent, I have tried to discover God's plan to save nations and peoples that we learn about from divine revelation, from the word proclaimed here at mass. Today, different historical solutions are proposed for our people. We can be sure that victory will go to the one that best reflects God's plan. The church's mission is to help that victory along. That is why, in light of the divine word that reveals God's plan for people's happiness, we have the duty, dear brothers and sisters, to point out facts that show how the plan of God is being reflected or distorted in our midst.

Let no one be offended because we use the divine words read at our mass to shed light on the social, political and economic situation of our people. Not to do so would be un-Christian. Christ desires to unite himself with humanity, so that the light he brings from God might become life for nations and individuals.

I know many are shocked by this preaching and want to accuse us of forsaking the gospel for politics. But I reject this accusation. I am trying to bring to life the message of the Second Vatican Council and the meetings at Medellin and Puebla. The documents from these meetings should not just be studied theoretically. They should be brought to life and translated into the real struggle to preach the gospel as it should be for our people. Each week I go about the country listening to the cries of the people, their pain from so much crime, and the ignominy of so much violence. Each week I ask the Lord to give me the right words to console, to denounce, to call for repentance. And even though I may be a voice crying in the desert, I know that the church is making the effort to fulfill its mission.

Here's a summary of that plan of God we've heard on these Lenten Sundays:

— Christ is the way. That is why he is presented to us fasting and conquering temptations in the desert. Christ is the goal and the life, the spur: that is why he appeared to us transfigured, to call us to that goal to which everyone is called.

— The collaboration of humanity is conversion. On the other Sundays of Lent — the third and fourth — we learned that God asks people to collaborate with him to be saved. The collaboration that God asks of people is conversion, reconciliation with him. In the precious examples of the fruitless fig tree, of the prodigal son, and from this morning's example of the adulteress who repents and is pardoned, comes the invitation God gives to us. He tells us that we will find ourselves forgiven just as the father forgave the prodigal son, just as the Saviour forgave the adulteress. No sin goes unpardoned; hatred can be reconciled when we are converted and sincerely return to the Lord. That is the message of Lent!

God's plan is realised in history. The readings of Lent tell us how God works out his plan in history, to make the history of nations his history of salvation. Insofar as those peoples reflect the plan of God — to save us in Christ by conversion — they gain salvation and happiness. For that reason, the history of Israel is treated in the first reading for each Sunday of Lent. The Israelites are a paradigm people, an example even in their infidelities and sins, because from them we learn how God punished infidelities and sins. They are also the model of how God brings about the promise of salvation. We travel with Moses on the pilgrimage through the desert; with Joshua, we arrive to celebrate the first passover in the promised land.

And today, we are invited to a second exodus: the return from Babylon. This is a story each nation has to imitate. Every population may not be the same as Israel's but one element does exist in all peoples: a group that follows Christ. The people of God are not the entire population, naturally, but a group of the faithful.

The example of Israel returning from Babylon is precious to us this morning, when followers of Christ in the US have come to share with the followers of Christ here in El Salvador. Christians in the great nation to the north are the voice of the gospel against that society's injustices. They come to stand beside us in solidarity so that we, the people of God here in El

4

Salvador, may also know how to denounce with courage the injustices of our own society.

In the light of today's divine word, I am going to present a reflection on this theme: 'the church, a servant of personal, communitarian and transcendent liberation'. These are the three main thoughts of today's homily: human dignity is the first thing freedom demands; God wants to save all peoples; and transcendence gives liberation its true and definitive dimension.

The dignity of the person

Look at the gospel. I find no more beautiful example of Jesus safeguarding human dignity than this sinless Jesus face to face with an adulteress, humiliated because she has been caught in adultery. Her judges sentence her to be stoned to death. Jesus silently reproaches her judges in their sin, asks the woman, 'Has no one condemned you?'

'No one, Lord.'

'Well, neither do I condemn you, but sin no more.'

Christ has strength and tenderness. He puts human dignity before all. There was a legal problem in the time of Christ. According to Deuteronomy, every woman caught in adultery was to die. When it came time to discuss how she ought to die, the pharisees and the lawyers debated: 'By stoning, by strangulation?' And they referred the question to Jesus: 'This woman has been caught in adultery. Our law says that she ought to die. What do *you* say? According to the present discussion, how should we kill her?'

These legal details were not important to Jesus. In answer to the malice of those laying a trap for him, Jesus began to write in the sand in an aimless way, like doodling on paper with a pencil. They insisted on an answer and Jesus gave them the great answer from his wisdom: 'Let the one among you who is without sin be the first to throw a stone'.

He touched their consciences. According to the ancient laws, they were witnesses, the ones that should have thrown the first stone. But in examining their consciences, the witnesses found they were witnesses of their own sins. So the dignity of the woman is saved. God does not save sin, but the dignity of a woman submerged in sin. Yes, God does save that. Jesus loves sinners; he has come precisely to save them, and here is an example of his doing that. To convert the adulteress is much better than to stone her; to pardon her and save her are much better than to condemn her. The law has to promote human dignity and must not use false legalities to trample upon the integrity of persons.

The gospel records the spontaneous reaction of the crowd: 'They started to fall away, beginning with the oldest'. Life is spent offending God, and the years slip by that ought to strengthen our commitment, to humanity, to human dignity, to God. We become more and more hypocritical, hiding the sins that increase with age.

Personal sin is the root of great social sin. Dear brothers and sisters, we must be very clear on this point because today it is very easy, as it was for the witnesses against the adulteress, to point out one sinner and yet to beg justice for others. But how few look at their own consciences! How easy it is to denounce structural injustice, institutionalised violence, social sin! All that is a reality, but where are the roots of that social sin? In the heart of every human being. Today's society is a kind of anonymous world in which no one wants to take the blame and everyone is responsible. Everyone is responsible for social sin, but its source is anonymous. We are all sinners and we have all added our grain of sand to the massive crime and violence in our country.

For that reason, salvation begins with the human person, with human dignity, with freeing every person from sin. And in Lent, this is God's call: be converted, individually! There are no two identical sinners among us. Each one of us has committed his or her own shameful deeds, yet we want to lay the blame on someone else and hide our own faults. I must unmask myself. I, too, am one of them, and I need to beg God's pardon because I have offended him and society. This is the call of Christ: the human person comes before all else —

How beautiful is the expression of that woman upon finding herself pardoned and understood. 'No one, Lord. No one has condemned me'.

'Then neither do I, I who could give that truly condemning word, neither do I condemn. But be careful. Do not sin again'. Do not sin again! Let us be careful, brothers and sisters. Since God has forgiven us so many times, let us take advantage of that friendship with the Lord which we have recovered and let us live it gratefully.

A note on the advancement of women: how beautifully a chapter on the promotion of woman by Christianity would fit in here! If she has achieved heights similar to man's much of this is due to the gospel of Jesus Christ. In the time of Christ, people were shocked that he would speak to a Samaritan woman because a woman was considered unworthy to speak to a man. Jesus knows that we are all equal, that there is no longer Greek nor Jew, man nor woman. We are all children of God. Women should be doubly appreciated by Christianity because Christ is the one who has encouraged the greatness of women. What heights women are capable of, when they use those feminine gifts that are often neither encouraged nor appreciated because of the machismo of men!

The witnesses must also understand that salvation begins with human dignity. Before being judges who administer justice, they have to be honest people who can pass sentence with a clean conscience because they would be the first to apply it to themselves if they were to commit that crime. Jesus' attitude is what we must focus on in this gospel, what we must learn. A sensitivity toward the person, however sinful that person may be, is what distinguishes him as the Son of God, the image of the Father. He does not condemn, but pardons. However, he does not tolerate sin. He is strong in rejecting sin, but he knows how to condemn the sin and save the sinner. He does not subordinate the person to the law. And this is very important in our own times. He says, 'The human person was not made for the Sabbath, but the Sabbath was made for humanity'.

Let us not call upon our country's constitution to defend our acts of selfishness, using it for our own interests. The law has already been abused everywhere. The law is for the benefit of the human person, not the person for the law. Jesus has given human dignity its rightful place, and we feel peace in that fact. We feel that we can count on Jesus, that we are not bound by sin, that we can repent and return to Jesus with sincerity. This is the deepest joy of being human.

In today's second reading, we have another example of a sinner who went about fooling himself for a long time. But in coming to know Christ he was saved and placed all his dreams, the aim of his whole life, in Christ.

'And everything else has become as nothing to me', the epistle says to us today. When the things of earth are no longer idolised, when we know the true God, the true Saviour, then all earthly ideologies, all worldly strategies, all the idols of power, of money, of material possessions, become as nothing to us. St Paul uses an even stronger word, 'manure'. He says, 'As long as I can win Christ, all the rest seems like manure to me'.

When we bishops met in Puebla, we issued a statement on the human person. So as not to keep you too long, brothers and sisters, I won't read the whole rich content of the Puebla document on the theological foundations of the dignity of persons. Let me just discuss three theological themes from Puebla: the truth about Christ; the truth about the church; and the truth about the human person.

As bishops of the continent we signed a document there, committing ourselves to promoting the human person. We spoke about the false earthly visions which make the human person an instrument of exploitation, or those visions in Marxist ideologies which make the person but a cog in the machinery, or those visions which make national security a servant of the state, as though the state were master and the people slaves, when the reverse is true. Humanity does not exist for the state, but rather the state exists for humanity. The ideal of promoting the person must be the highest aim of all human organisation.

We, the bishops of Latin America, have committed ourselves:

> We profess, then, that every man and every woman, no matter how insignificant they may seem, has within themselves an inviolable nobility that they and all others ought to respect unconditionally; that each human life deserves to be treated with dignity for its own sake, under whatever circumstance; that all human coexistence has to be based on the common good, on the realisation of the increasingly severe reprimand the common dignity makes against injustice. The common dignity does not permit using some persons for the pleasure of others, but demands that people should be prepared to sacrifice particular goods.

This is the basis of our sociology, that which we learn from Christ in his gospel: before all else, the human being is what we have to save, and individual sin is the first thing we have to correct. Our personal accounts before God, our individual relationship with him, set the stage for everything else. False liberators are people whose souls are slaves to sin but who clamour for justice. They are often cruel because they know neither how to love nor how to respect the human person.

God wants to save everyone

In moving from the individual to the communitarian, we come to the second theme for this homily. The idea is presented beautifully in today's readings, which show how God desires to save people as a group. It is the whole population God wants to save.

Today's first reading, the famous poem of Isaiah, presents God speaking with a people. Isaiah records the dialogue of God with what is called a 'corporate personality', as though God were speaking with one person. God speaks with a people and to that people. God makes them his people because he is going to entrust them with promises, revelations that soon will serve for all peoples.

There is a difference between 'people of God' and all people. Mark my words, beloved brothers and sisters: in the bible, there are things that apply only to the 'people of God', and there are also some things that apply to people in general, to all people. How many times the prophets reproached Israel for delighting in being children of Abraham without obeying and believing in God. The believers, that diminished number, were the true people of God. At times, all the rest were corrupt and so, too, were the other people who were called the Gentiles. But that nucleus called the people of God, the corporate person with whom God speaks, works through Christ to make all people Christians. No longer is there only one group of people of God from Israel; now there are also many groups of people of God.

Here this morning we have an example. There is a group of Christians in the United States that does not include all people there, just as in El Salvador there is a group of Christians that does not include all of El Salvador's people. And when I, as pastor, address the people of God, I don't pretend to be the

9

master of all of El Salvador. I am the servant of a nucleus that is called the church, the archdiocese, those that want to serve Christ and who recognise the bishop as the teacher who speaks to them in the name of Christ.

From them I expect respect and obedience. With them I have such a bond that it doesn't bother me that those who are not of the church, although some may be within it, criticise me, murmur at me, pick me apart. They are no longer the people of God. This is in line with the New Testament. Even though they may be baptised, even though they may come to mass, if they can't join in solidarity with the exacting teachings of the gospel and the specific applications of it in our ministry, then, brothers and sisters, let us make a careful distinction so as not to cheapen that sacred name, the people. When we appeal to the people of God, we appeal to the nucleus of Salvadoreans who believe in Christ and want to follow him faithfully, who are nourished by his life, by his sacraments, around his pastors.

God saves in history

This people of God exists throughout history. Did you notice what today's reading says so beautifully? 'You were glorified by the first exodus, when I took you out of Egypt, when you cross-ed the desert. How many marvellous deeds were done on that journey with Moses! But glory no longer in that past! Already, that has become history. I make all things new'. What a beautiful phrase from God! It is God who makes all things new; it is God who goes on in history.

Isaiah says the exodus will now come from another direction, from Babylon, from exile. The desert through which the people are going to pass will flower like a garden; the waters will gush forth, symbolising the giving of God's pardon. The people will be reconciled with God on the way to Jerusalem. The exodus is no longer from the slavery of Egypt, but from the desert of Babylon. And so history will go on unfolding.

Every country lives its own 'exodus'; today El Salvador is living its own exodus. Today we are passing to our liberation through a desert strewn with bodies and where anguish and pain are devastating us. Many suffer the temptation of those who walked with Moses and wanted to turn back and did not work together. It is the same old story. God, however, wants to save the people by making a new history. History does not repeat itself, although there is a saying to that effect. Obviously, there are certain phenomena that are repeated. What is not a repetition of past history is the circumstance, the precise moment to which we are witnesses in El Salvador.

How complicated is our history, how varied from one day to another! One leaves El Salvador and returns the following week, and it seems that the history of the country has changed completely. Let us not judge things as we once judged them. One thing is important: let us keep our faith in Jesus Christ, the God of history, firmly anchored in our souls. That does not change. But Christ has, as it were, the satisfaction of changing history, of influencing history: 'I make all things new'.

The grace of the Christian, therefore, must not be based on traditions that no longer sustain themselves, but must apply that eternal tradition of Christ to the present realities. We have to have changes in the church, dear brothers and sisters, a fact that applies above all to those of us who have been formed at other times, in other systems. We have to ask God for the grace to adapt ourselves without betraying our faith, to understand the present movement. God makes all things new. He punished the Israelites because, glorying in the first exodus, they did not think God could perform marvels in a second exodus or that he would do greater things in the Christian era, as we ourselves are seeing.

History will not fail; God sustains it. That is why I say that insofar as historical projects attempt to reflect the eternal plan of God, to that extent they reflect the kingdom of God. This attempt is the work of the church. Because of this, the church, the people of God in history, is not attached to any one social system, to any political organisation, to any party. The church does not identify herself with any of those forces because she is the eternal pilgrim of history and is indicating at every historical moment what reflects the kingdom of God and what does not reflect the kingdom of God. She is the servant of the kingdom of God.

The great task of Christians must be to absorb the spirit of God's kingdom and, with souls filled with the kingdom of God, to work on the projects of history. It's fine to be organised in popular groups; it's all right to form political parties; it's all right to take part in the government. It's fine as long as you are a Christian who carries the reflection of the kingdom of God and tries to establish it where you are working, and as long as you are not being used to further worldly ambitions. This is the great duty of the people of today. My dear Christians, I have always told you, and I will repeat, that the true liberators of our people must come from us Christians, from the people of God. Any historical plan that's not based on what we spoke of in the first point — the dignity of the human being, the love of God, the kingdom of Christ among people — will be a fleeting project. Your project, however, will grow in stability the more it reflects the eternal design of God. It will be a solution for the common good of the people every time, if it meets the needs of the people.

We must be grateful for the church, dear political brothers and sisters, and not manipulate the church into saying what we want; instead, we must say what the church teaches. The church doesn't have interests. I do not have any ambition for power. Because of that, I freely tell the powerful people what is good and what is bad. I also tell any political group what is good and what is bad. That is my duty.

Having that freedom of the kingdom of God, we, the church (which is not only the bishop and the priests, but all of you, the faithful, the religious, the Catholic schools, all who are the people of God, the nucleus of believers in Christ), should unify our efforts. We should not be divided or appear disunited. We often seem to have a complex about the popular political organisations, and we want to please them, rather than the kingdom of God in its eternal designs. We don't have to go begging to anyone because we have much to give everyone. This is not arrogance, but the grateful humility of people who have received a revelation from God to communicate to others.

Transcendence and liberation
Finally, the third thought taken from today's readings is that the plan of God for liberating his people is transcendent.

I think I may repeat this idea too often, but I'll never tire of saying it because we often run the risk of wanting to get out of present situations with immediate resolutions, and we forget that quick answers can be makeshift remedies, but not true solutions. The true solution has to fit into the definitive plan of God. Every effort we make for better land distribution, for better administration of wealth in El Salvador, for a political organisation structured around the common good of Salvadoreans, will always have to be made within the context of definitive liberation.

Recently, I was taught a very important idea. It is that one who works in politics looks at temporal problems such as money, land and things, and is content with simply solving these problems. But the politician who has faith goes to God, and from God's point of view looks at that immediate problem which the politicians are trying to solve. The problem should not be considered apart from God's perspective.

From the beginning to the end of history, God has a plan; for any solution to be effective, it must be moulded according to that perspective of God. And according to God's perspective, as it appears in today's readings from the Bible, three things are clear: in the first place, we must recognise God as the shaper of history; in the second place, we must break out of bondage to sin; and in the third place, we must not reject Christ, who is the way and the goal of true liberation. There it is in today's reading. This is the plan we have been studying through Lent.

First, we must recognise God's initiative in order to liberate our people. Today's readings clearly show that God is the one who takes the initiative. In the first reading, God speaks of 'the people that I formed'. It is God speaking with Israel: 'I chose you: I am making your history for you'. The moment we understand that we are no more than instruments of God is a beautiful one.

Whatever lives comes from God. We can do only as much as God wants us to do; we have only as much intelligence as God has given us. We must place all those limitations in God's hands and recognise that without God we can do nothing. My beloved brothers and sisters, with that sense of transcendence, we are called to pray much, to be closely united with God at this hour in El Salvador. There are people who are working for liberation by uniting themselves with God.

The other day we were speaking about the problem of the refugee camp. Do not confuse the refugee camp with a barracks; the refugee camp is for people who come with fear and who come fleeing, trying to hide themselves. People say, 'Lots of people are organised. We can't sit doing nothing — we have to work!' All right, go and work. Look for a barracks to work in. But the refugee camp is a place where even sick people work. There was a father with his sick wife and his children. They were helpless, but they wanted to send them to occupy a church. How can someone do that if they are sick? Let them offer their suffering, their illness. That is valuable, but when people lose sight of the transcendence of the struggle everything is reduced to things which are sometimes wrong. Would that all those who are working now for the liberation of the people would realise that without God nothing is possible and that with God even the most useless thing is work when done with good will.

In today's first reading, God invites the people of Israel to discover his hand, not only in their exodus from Egypt to the promised land, but also in their return from Babylon to Jerusalem. To see the hand of God in the historical reality of that people is to experience transcendence. Those who work — I repeat — for the liberation of the people should not lose sight of this transcendent dimension.

The second point about the transcendent nature of liberation is this: we must remember that liberation must free us from sin. We must bear in mind that all evils have a common root. It is sin. In the human heart are egotism, envy, idolatry, and from these come divisions and avarice. As Christ said, 'It is not what comes out of persons that defiles them, but rather what is in the human heart: evil thoughts'.

We must purify, then, that source of all bondage. Why are there chains? Why are there 'marginal' people? Why is there illiteracy? Why are there diseases? Why do people mourn in pain? All of that indicates that sin does exist. 'The poverty of a people', says Medellín, 'is a denunciation of the injustice that people endures'.

Liberation, because it is transcendent, lifts us out of our sins. The church will always be preaching, 'Repent of your personal sins'. And she will say, as Christ did to the adulteress, 'I do not condemn you; you have repented, but do not sin again'. Brothers and sisters, all of you who think little of an intimate relationship with God, how much I want to convince you how important God is! It is not enough to say, I'm an atheist, or, I

14

don't believe in God, or, I don't offend him. It is not a question of what you believe. Objectively you have broken with the source of life. As long as you don't discover this, don't follow him, and don't love him, you are cut off from your creator. And because of this, you carry within yourself disorder, disunity, ingratitude, lack of faith, lack of community. Without God, there is no true liberation. Granted, one may achieve temporary liberations. But definitive, lasting liberations — only people of faith are going to realise them.

The third idea on the transcendent aspect of liberation is that transcendence asks of us great faith in Jesus Christ. Today's second reading gives us an incomparable page from the life of St Paul, the sinner who had forgotten Christ or, rather, did not know him and believed instead that Christ and his Christians were traitors to the true religion, judaism. Paul felt authorised to persecute them, arrest them and wipe them out.

But when Christ revealed himself to Paul, Paul understood his own ignorance. Thus he wrote, 'All that I esteemed I now count as loss compared to the excellence of knowing Jesus Christ, my Lord'. What gratitude from a sinner! Paul says, 'I didn't know you, Lord; now, yes, now I know you and now all the rest seems useless to me compared to the excellence of knowing you, my Lord! For Christ, I lost everything. And all I esteemed I count as refuse, in order that I may gain Christ and be found in him, not having a righteousness of my own but with that justice which comes from faith in Christ'. This is transcendence.

There are many who want justice, their own justice, a simple human justice. They do not go beyond that. That is not what saves me, says St Paul; rather, justice comes from faith in Christ, my Lord. And how is Christ judge of humanity? St Paul hopes 'to know Christ and the strength of his resurrection and to share his sufferings, becoming like him in his death that I may attain one day the resurrection of the dead'.

Do you see how life recovers all of its meaning? Do you see how suffering becomes a communion with the Christ who suffers, and death becomes a communion with the death that redeemed the world? Who can feel worthless before this treasure that one finds in Christ, that gives meaning to sickness, to pain, to oppression and repression? Whoever believes in

15

Christ, even under the oppressor's boot, knows that he or she is a victor and that the definitive victory will be that of truth and justice!

In the same intimate passage, St Paul says, 'The most important thing is not what I've already acquired, but rather that I rush forward, forgetting what remains behind and driving myself towards that which is ahead. I run toward the goal in order to win the prize of God's heavenly call in Jesus Christ'. This is transcendence: the goal toward which we strive with each step of liberation, a goal that is definitive joy for all people.

Events of the week

Brothers and sisters, this transcendent liberation is the liberation our church has to live and preach. We have already learned it from the word of God on the eve of Holy Week. And we are going to enter into Holy Week forming ourselves more into the church, the people of God.

I speak at this moment to my beloved priests, to the religious communities, to the Christian communities, to all who are called the church, the people of God, the nucleus of believers, in order that from here, from this core of believers, we might have the strength (as God gave it to Israel) to enlighten all other peoples, to expose and denounce that which is not good, and to encourage all that is good. For that reason, at this point in my homily, I am directing myself to the task of our church, asking of all church workers to truly make the church a vehicle of the liberation called for in the plan of God.

The first thing I announce to you today is that next Sunday we begin Holy Week. Because of special circumstances we are going to celebrate it here, in the basilica. At 8 a.m. next Sunday, we'll have the blessing of the palms. We hope to combine our service with that of the Church of Calvary. In that case, I am asking you to be in the Church of Calvary at about 7.30 a.m. where we will bless the palms. From there, we will have a procession — which symbolises the triumphal entrance of Christ into Jerusalem — to the entrance of the basilica to celebrate Palm Sunday mass.

The rest of the events of Holy Week will appear on the programme. The first major celebration comes on Holy Thursday, with the blessing of the oils at 10 a.m., but we will announce all

16

of this next Sunday. I only want to tell you ahead of time that we would like to give our Good Friday Way of the Cross its full meaning of reparation, of denunciation and of solidarity, the three attitudes with which a Christian should meditate on the passion of Christ. We live among a people who shoulder their own heavy cross. Next Sunday, we will give you the details for this celebration of the great way of the cross that is truly one with the way of the cross of our own people.

Let me mention various communities in the archdiocese. As I already told you last Sunday, the celebration of the feast of St Joseph proved to be very prayerful in San José de la Montana, in the seminaries under his patronage, in San José Cortes, in San José Villanueva, in Christopher Columbus Academy — directed by the Josephine fathers — and in the St Joseph day school.

In Aguilares, we celebrated the third anniversary of Father Rutilio Grande's assassination. The repression is obviously having its effect — few people were present; there is fear. One could say the people of Aguilares are being martyred. The message was that Christ's messenger will always meet the fate Father Grande met if the messenger is faithful.

In Tejutla, in the village of Los Martinez, we celebrated the village feast day. And there they told me of a terrible violation of human rights. On 7 March about midnight, a truckful of soldiers, some in mufti and some in uniform, opened doors, entered homes, and set upon all the members of each family, violently kicking them and beating them with rifle butts. The soldiers raped four young women, savagely beat up their parents, and threatened that if they said anything about it they would have to bear the consequences. We have learned of the tragedy of these poor young girls.

In Agua Caliente, we had a beautiful confirmation ceremony — the people are very kind there in the district of Chalatenango, in the parish of Mary Queen of Heaven.

In Cojutepeque, the parish priest, Father Richard Ayala, has been the victim of a false denunciation. This telegram arrived at the chancery, a copy of a telegram from the commander of the National Guard to the head of the general staff:

I have the honour to forward to you this radio communication originating this date from the Cojutepeque National

17

Guard. The communication reads, 'From the commander, National Police. Am communicating by telephone that this headquarters has learned that toward the end of last week, Father Richard Ayala, parish priest of San Sebastian Church in this city, met with groups of people of both sexes in the village of San Andres, in the jurisdiction of Monte San Juan in this district, to report to them that on the 15th of this month he will leave for Nicaragua or for Cuba to bring reinforcements to continue the revolt in our country'.

The commander signed the telegram.

Ridiculous, isn't it?

When we called on Father Ayala, whom many know for his seriousness, he wrote this to the engineer Duarte, who sent the telegram to me at the curia:

On the subject of the telegram, I tell you this: first, it is true that on the date indicated I was in the villages of El Carmen and Soledad in the jurisdiction of Monte San Juan, and I was accompanied by Father Benjamin Rodriguez, a parish priest from that area; second, our visit was intended to reconcile and console both factions with religious words and the gospel; and third, it is completely false and biased to assert that we may have offered to leave the country on the 15th of the present month to bring back reinforcements from other countries in order to continue the right. That is *not* our language, nor is that the pastoral mission which has been entrusted to us. Sincerely, Father Ayala.

In another community of the Cuscatlán district, in Candelaria, it is reported that the National Guard in the villages of San Miguel, Nance Verde and San Juan Miraflores Arriba — with the understanding of officials in Candelaria, Cuscatlán — in the afternoon hours arrested a young reservist, Emilio Mejía, who was with other people in a bus going towards Cojutepeque. He was taken to his village, San José La Ceiba, where that same afternoon he was killed in front of the house of Don Salvador Mejía. There his body was picked up by his mother, Doña Carmen Martinez de Mejía, on the morning of the following day and he was buried that afternoon. Some say that this happened by mistake; the police were looking for another person with the same name. A fatal mistake.

Second, Mr Emilio Mejía was arrested in his own home in the village of San Juan Miraflores Arriba, in front of his wife, Doña Pilar Raymundo de Mejía, and after being abused, he was taken from the house. The following day, his wife found him about two blocks away, decapitated. Third, arrested, in their home in the village of San Miguel Nance Verde were Don José Cupertino Alvarado and his daughters, Carmen Alvarado and María Josefa Alvarado. They were found dead on a coffee plantation behind the chapel in the village of San Juan Miraflores Arriba. The following day, they were buried in a common grave by their relatives. Fourth, it is on record that all of the dead were arrested peacefully in their homes — with the exception of the first one (young Emilio Mejía) — without offering resistance. The signatory of this statement saw a bus full of National Guardsmen in front of the ANTEL office in the afternoon hours.

The statement offers a beautiful legal analysis; the signatory makes it very clear that the law, in addition to people's lives, has been trampled upon. One of his paragraphs says, 'By the present declaration, I am not defending anarchy or subversion if in fact the dead have been accused of such things, but rather I am calling into question this lawless conduct completely opposed to the dignity of human persons'.

In response to our chancery's protest at the seizure of the Belgian fathers' house on the Zacamil settlement, the Ministry of Defence has answered,

As regards the seizure of the house named, I want to offer the following details for your consideration: first, that it has no sign to identify it as the house of priests or as a place of religious worship; second, that not only was that house seized but also another in the same area because there were reports that merited investigation — that is to say, that the second house seized was suspect, as was that of the fathers . . .; third, that as soon as it was verified that the house belonged to priests and that nothing suspicious had been found, the seizure was suspended; fourth, that the possibility is not being dismissed that after the seizures other persons may have entered the house interested in doing damage or in leaving the impression that the seizure

19

was violent.

I admit that upon questioning the members of the National Guard about the incident at hand, they did not deny that the seizure was carried out. We ordered them to have more care and consideration for special cases like the one noted, and ordered that we be consulted before they act.

Alas, the events tell a different story!

The following announcements will help keep you informed about the life of our diocese. We will have confirmations at 4pm today on Real Ciudad Delgado Street.

This week, the catechumenal communities will celebrate the proclamation of Easter.

In Soyapango, a new Christian centre, directed by the Dominican Fathers of the Rosary, has been opened.

In Santa Tecla the basic ecclesial community is studying and committing itself ever more firmly to this pastoral approach.

In Chalatenango, a new parish is growing up: Christ the King Parish, formed to serve Paraíso, Aldeíta and Chalatenango. The pastor will be Father Gabriel Rodríguez. The parish will be staffed by four seminarians spending their diaconate year there, in preparation for their coming priesthood.

The educational communities too are doing pastoral work in the Catholic high schools, which gives us every hope that the work of the schools will not be merely parallel, and certainly not opposed, to the pastoral strategy of the archdiocese. We have had meetings with the lay staff of Assumption and are going to have meetings with those of Sacred Heart.

Two diocesan organisations are renewing their membership; they are the Pastoral Council and nine area vicars. They have spent two days this week studying, concentrating on the archdiocese's pastoral plan, which is — and keep this clearly in mind so that you are not surprised by incorrect reports — a response to the ideas of Vatican II, to the Medellin and Puebla meetings and to the pastoral weeks held in our archdiocese.

I do not like it when people refer to the 'thinking of the archbishop'. I have no personal 'line'; rather, I try to follow the line of the great events of the church. And I am delighted that the pastoral commission studies documents such as the diocese's plan, which I already received, like a precious heritage, from Monsignor Chávez, a plan we are trying to put into practice. We are having great success with it in the communities that take it seriously.

The priests' senate also named its new executive. It is an organisation whose work is to serve every priest and the whole diocese.

Our special thanks go to Father Pick and his collaborators who have worked so hard to get the broadcasting station working, the station that allows people from far away to listen to our message.

The gesture of solidarity made by our North American Christian brothers and sisters is not isolated. I have learned that in North America many statements from Christian groups expressed sympathy for the letter we sent to the president of the United States. These groups support our desire for him not to give military help that contributes to the repression of our people. One of those statements of support is an article signed by Mr Murat Williams, who was US ambassador here in El Salvador during the time of President Rivera. He confirms, from his experience, that such aid from the United states always ends up being used for military repression here in El Salvador.

Because there can be confusion about certain events, our information office has prepared two clarifications.

The first one refers to the policeman tortured in the cathedral. The official version leaves the role of our archbishopric a little ambiguous. It says that people sought help from the archbishopric and that the result was negative. This wording is dangerous; we never fail to pay attention when action is needed, and we always do what we can. The bulletin explains:

On 21 March, members of FAPU requested that the archbishopric help them with the burial of 17 bodies that they had in the cathedral because they were afraid of being stopped on the way to the cemetery. Because of that, they had to bury the dead in the cathedral. The archbishopric promised to obtain guarantees for the burial. That was successfully carried out through the Ministry of Defence, which paid close attention to the case, arranging the par-

21

ticipation of the International Red Cross and requesting the participation of the Ministry of Public Health.

The arrangements made on behalf of the archbishopric were communicated to the representatives of the organisations, FAPU and BPR, but the representatives disagreed on what action to take. Some favoured taking the dead to the cemetery and the others said they should be buried in the cathedral. The representatives of the archbishopric, as well as the members of the International Red Cross, said they would collaborate in a normal burial, but would not assist in the show of protest that the organisations might be expected to make on this occasion.

When these arrangements were made, Colonel Reynaldo López Nuila, director of the National Police, requested by telephone the intervention of the archbishop's office to get the occupants of the cathedral to free Corporal Miguel Angel Zúñiga, whom they had seized. The archbishop immediately sent a delegate to the cathedral. The occupiers paid the delegate no attention, and they denied having Corporal Zúñiga there. Later, with a member of Legal Aid, the delegate went to the University of El Salvador to speak with the Revolutionary Co-ordinating Committee.

There, they were informed that the corporal had certainly been captured but that they had freed him. At the same time, with representatives of the International Red Cross, they talked about the burial of the bodies. In this discussion it was decided that the BPR would bury its members in the cemetery, and FAPU would bury its members in the cathedral.

Secondly, a commission of priests and lay people presented themselves at the Military Hospital to speak with Corporal Miguel Angel Zúñiga. He told them that when he was passing in front of the cathedral, four individuals armed with submachine guns approached him. They brought him into the cathedral, took him to the basement, where they beat him and put iron rings round the wrists and hands and gave him electric shocks. They beat him about the eyes and stomach, demanding that he tell them the names of his superiors and companions, as well as the numbers of their vehicles. They said he should report all of this information to the national university.

One of those who interrogated him sprayed his eyes with a liquid that smelled of sulphur and gave him great pain and a fierce burning sensation. They told him that if he didn't co-operate they would treat him as the people of San Martín had been treated, and they said they would kill his mother. They held guns to his head. He swore to them by God and his mother than he had never tortured or done harm to anyone. At last, they pushed him out in the street where he got a taxi. The doctor that attended him at the hospital said that for the time being Corporal Zúñiga could not see, but that the doctors hoped he would regain his sight. Two of his fingers are paralysed because of the electric shocks.

This is what happened to the policeman. On no account can we approve of such cruelty. Human beings are the highest entity we can conceive of, and must be respected.

The other case we want to clarify is this: the Catholic Church has opened four buildings it owns to shelter refugees who have fled their homes because of the violence afflicting many places in this country. Our church is fully aware that protecting with care anyone who suffers is one of its principal obligations; we should not take into account the person's creed or political persuasion or way of thinking. For the church, it is enough simply to know a person is coming for help. The church has set aside four sites for refuge, not for centres of political indoctrination of any sort, and by no means for military training camps that put people in danger instead of protecting them. The church has asked the popular organisations to respect the strict function of sheltering, the purpose that those places have assumed. This purpose has also been made known to the military authorities.

The church is carrying out this humanitarian work through Cáritas, the official organisation of the archdiocese for giving this kind of service. Aside from Cáritas, the church does not recognise any other organisation as a charitable agency officially representing the church. It remains very clear, then, that only Cáritas represents the archbishopric in these works of kindness, help and charity. Cáritas is a member of CEAH (Economic Committee of Humanitarian Aid) that unites, on an economic level, many organisations of concern. These other organisations, though, do not represent the Catholic Church; it is represented only by Cáritas. The archdiocese entrusts to Cáritas the duty of persevering in devoted intervention for the needy, through humanitarian and Christian endeavours. And if the efforts of Cáritas have not gained all the desired results, this has not been through inaction, but rather because it has not received the understanding and the collaboration necessary.

On a pleasant, note, let me mention something special done in our diocese: a composer and poet has written a beautiful hymn for us in honour of our divine Saviour. Now, listen to some lines from it:

The explosive songs of joy vibrate.
I am going to join
with the people in the cathedral . . .
thousands of voices, we unite on this day
to sing our patron's feast day.

The hymn includes stanzas very sensitive to what our people are undergoing. The last stanza is beautiful:

But the gods of power and money
are opposed to transfiguration.
Because of that, you support us now, Lord,
our leader against oppression.

I had some texts from the pope, which we are going to omit because I only brought them to confirm the doctrine we are preaching. Above all, the doctrine gives priority to respect for the human person.

National events

Now I invite you to look at things through the eyes of the church, which is trying to be the kingdom of God on earth and so often must illuminate the realities of our national situation.

We have lived through a tremendously tragic week. I could not give you the facts before, but a week ago last Saturday, on 15 March, one of the largest and most distressing military operations was carried out in the countryside. The villages affected were La Laguna, Plan de Ocotes and El Rosario. The operation brought tragedy: a lot of ranches were burned, there was looting, and — inevitably — people were killed. In La Laguna, the attackers killed a married couple, Ernesto Navas and Audelia Mejía de Navas, their little children, Martin and Hilda, 13 and seven years old, and 11 more peasants.

Other deaths have been reported, but we do not know the names of the dead. In Plan de Ocotes, two children and four peasants were killed, including two women. In El Rosario, three more peasants were killed. That was last Saturday.

Last Sunday, the following were assassinated in Arcatao by four members of ORDEN: peasants Marcelino Serrano, Vincente Ayala, 24 years old and his son, Freddy. That same day, Fernando Hernandez Navarro, a peasant, was assassinated in Galera de Jutiapa, when he fled from the military.

Last Monday, 17 March, was a tremendously violent day. Bombs exploded in the capital as well as in the interior of the country. The damage was very substantial at the headquarters of the Ministry of Agriculture. The campus of the national university was under armed siege from dawn until 7 p.m. Throughout the day, constant bursts of machine-gun fire were heard in the university area. The archbishop's office intervened to protect people who found themselves caught inside.

On the Hacienda Colima, 18 persons died, at least 15 of whom were peasants. The administrator and the grocer of the ranch also died. The armed forces confirmed that there was a confrontation. A film of the events appeared on TV, and many analysed interesting aspects of the situation.

At least 50 people died in serious incidents that day: in the capital, seven persons died in events at the Colonia Santa Lucía; on the outskirts of Tecnillantas, five people died; and in the area of the rubbish dump, after the evacuation of the site by the military, were found the bodies of four workers who had been captured in that action.

Sixteen peasants died in the village of Montepeque, 38 kilometres along the road to Suchitoto. That same day, two students at the University of Central America were captured in Tecnillantas: Mario Nelson and Miguel Alberto Rodríguez Velado, who were brothers. The first one, after four days of illegal detention, was handed over to the courts. Not so his brother, who was wounded and is still held in illegal detention. Legal Aid is intervening on his behalf.

Amnesty International issued a press release in which it described the repression of the peasants, especially in the area of

Chalatenango. The week's events confirm this report in spite of the fact the government denies it. As I entered the church, I was given a cable that says, 'Amnesty International confirmed today (that was yesterday) that in El Salvador human rights are violated to extremes that have not been seen in other countries'. That is what Patricio Fuentes (spokesman for the urgent action section for Central America in Swedish Amnesty International) said at a press conference in Managua, Nicaragua.

Fuentes confirmed that, during two weeks of investigations he carried out in El Salvador, he was able to establish that there had been 83 political assassinations between 10 and 14 March. He pointed out that Amnesty International recently condemned the government of El Salvador, alleging that it was responsible for 600 political assassinations. The Salvadorean government defended itself against the charges, arguing that Amnesty International based its condemnation on unproved assumptions.

Fuentes said that Amnesty had established that in El Salvador human rights are violated to a worse degree than the repression in Chile after the coup d'état. The Salvadorean government also said that the 600 dead were the result of armed confrontations between army troops and guerrillas. Fuentes said that during his stay in El Salvador, he could see that the victims had been tortured before their deaths and mutilated afterwards.

The spokesman of Amnesty International said that the victims' bodies characteristically appeared with the thumbs tied behind their back. Corrosive liquids had been applied to the corpses to prevent identification of the victims by their relatives and to prevent international condemnation, the spokesman added. Nevertheless, the bodies were exhumed and the dead have been identified. Fuentes said that the repression carried out by the Salvadorean army was aimed at breaking the popular organisations through the assassination of their leaders in both town and country.

According to the spokesman of Amnesty International, at least 3,500 peasants have fled from their homes to the capital to escape persecution. 'We have complete lists in London and Sweden of young children and women who have been assassinated for being organised', Fuentes stated.

He said that Amnesty International is a humanitarian organisation that does not align itself with governments, organisations or persons. 'We do not reject the government, but we do strive to make human rights respected in every part of the world . . . especially where they are most threatened or crushed', said Fuentes. Well, this confirms what we have been saying about this frightful week.

I would like to analyse what may be the cause of those violent acts: the work stoppage called for by the Revolutionary Co-ordinating Committee (RCM).

The purpose of the strike is to protest against the repression. Last Sunday, I said that purpose is legitimate, because it denounces something that cannot be tolerated. But the stoppage also had a political intention, to show that instead of intimidating the popular organisations, the repression was building them up. The intention was to reject opposition from the present government which is forced to resort to violent repression to carry out its reforms. Some of those reforms, for various reasons, are not acceptable to the popular organisations.

The state of siege and the misinformation to which we are subject — through official communiqués as well as through most of the media — do not yet allow us to measure objectively the extent of the general strike. Foreign broadcasts have reported a 70 per cent work stoppage, which would certainly be a very high percentage and could be considered a notable triumph. Not even counting the establishments that closed for fear of both actions from the left and those carried out by the right and the government in the early hours of that same Monday, it cannot be denied that the power demonstrated by the RCM in the country, strictly in terms of labour, was great. The RCM is strong not only in the countryside, but also in the factories and in the city.

Very probably mistakes were made, but in spite of all those faults it can be judged that that stoppage was an advance in the popular struggle and a demonstration that the left can paralyse the economic activity of the country. The government's answer to the stoppage, granted, was hard. Not only did surveillance throughout the city and the wild shooting at the University of El Salvador demonstrate that, but above all the deaths that occur-

27

red. No less than 10 workers from the factories on strike were killed by agents of the security forces and three workers from the town hall were found murdered after having been detained by the Treasury Police. This is a clear condemnation of the administration in our own capital

But these deaths were matched by others on the same day, numbering at least 60, according to some people; others say there were more than 140. Moreover, it is to be noted that the work stoppage in the countryside was accompanied by the aggressive activities of a few popular organisations. Examples are Colima, San Martín and Suchitoto. The tactics of these organisations' operations might be questioned, but their questionableness certainly does not justify the repressive action of the government.

Certainly the Co-ordinating Committee has its faults; it needs to change a great deal to become a coherent alternative example of democratic revolutionary power. They must take stock and carry on working out a way of being the genuine expression of the people and not engage in wild actions which are repudiated by the people. There is hope for a solution if they become mature and manage genuinely to incorporate the people's wishes.

It is not true that their failures result from their being subversives, evil or antisocial. Their failures result from their not being allowed a normal political development. They are persecuted, massacred. It is made difficult for them to organise, to develop their links with other democratic groups. The result will be that they become more radical and desperate. In these circumstances it is difficult for them not to engage in revolutionary activities and violent struggles. The least that can be said is that the country is going through a pre-revolutionary stage and certainly not a stage of transition.

The fundamental question is how to find a less violent way out of this critical stage. On this point, the greatest responsibility belongs to the civil government, and above all, to the military. How I wish that they would not let themselves be blinded by what they are doing in agrarian reform. That can be a deception that prevents them from seeing the whole problem.

Tuesday — we continue to speak of the past week, a week weighed down by acts that cannot go unmentioned. In the clippings I brought here about the pope, he notes the number of victims that Italy has had during these days, especially in Rome. Well, since the pope pointed out the mere ten cruel assassinations in Italy, I'm sure if he were in my place, he would take time day by day (just as we are taking the time now) to speak of the many, many assassinations that occur here.

On 18 March, the bodies of four peasants were found in different areas — two in Metapán, two in San Miguel.

On Wednesday, 19 March, at 5.30am, after a military operation in the villages of San Luis La Loma, La Cayetana, León de Piedra, La India, Paz, Opico and El Mono, the bodies of three peasants were found: Humberto Urbino, Oswaldo Hernández and Francisco García.

In the capital at 2 p.m., the premises of both the Trade Union of Beverages and of the Revolutionary Trade Union Federation were occupied by the military. This happened when many workers were keeping watch over the body of Manuel Pacín, consultant for the municipal workers. After having been captured, Pacín was killed: his body was found in Apulo. The military operation resulted in the deaths of two persons, one of them a worker, Mauricio Batrera, leader of the engineering and metal-workers' union.

Nine peasants were killed in a confrontation in the town of San Bartolo Tecoluca, according to a report in the national press by the armed forces. At noon in the town of El Almendral, in the jurisdiction of Majagual, La Libertad, army soldiers captured three peasants — Miguel Angel Gomez de Paz, Concepción Coralia Menjívar and José Emilio Valencia. They have yet to be freed. We ask that they be handed over to the courts.

At 4 p.m. on Thursday 20 March, in the village of El Jocote, Quezaltepeque, a peasant leader named Alfonso Muñoz Pacheco was assassinated. The disputes secretary for the Federation of Rural Workers, peasant Muñoz was known widely in the country for his dedication to the cause of the peasants.

And something very terrible, very important, happened on this same day (Thursday, 20 March) — Agustín Sánchez, a peasant, was found still alive but critically wounded. On 15 March, he had been captured in Zacetecoluca by soldiers who handed him over to the local police. Peasant Sánchez has affirmed, in a declaration given before a notary and witnesses, that his capture occurred on the ranch of El Cauca, in the district of La Paz, where he was working in a branch of the Salvadorean Communal Union. The police detained him for four days, without food and water, torturing him with constant whippings and throttlings until 19 March, when they shot him and two other peasants in the head. Luckily, the bullet only shattered his right cheekbone and eye. Found near death in the early morning, he was helped by some peasants until a reliable person took him to this capital. Peasant Sánchez could not sign this appalling testimony because they had smashed both of his hands. Persons of recognised integrity witnessed his horrible condition, and there are photographs that reveal the state in which this poor peasant was picked up.

From San Pablo Tacachico, we had an unconfirmed report of the mass murder of 25 peasants. At the beginning of this mass, we received confirmation of this terrible tragedy. The report says that on 21 March from 6 a.m. on, a military operation took place on Santa Ana Street, which runs through San Pablo Tacachico. The operation mentioned was carried out by soldiers from the Opico and Santa Ana quarters, along with the treasury police assigned to Tacachico. They carried with them lists of names of persons to be searched. In the operation mentioned, the soldiers and police carried out a search in the villages of El Resbaladero, San Felipe, Moncagua, El Portillo, San José La Cova, Mogotes, and their respective settlements, Los Pozos and Las Delicias. The soldiers and police also took the names of all travellers by bus or on foot.

In the district of Mogotes, in the jurisdiction of Tacachico, the repression was most cruel, as the troops of soldiers, with two small tanks, spread terror among the inhabitants of this sector. In the search they carried out, four radios and 400 colónes in cash were stolen. The troops burned the home and all of the belongings of Rosalio Cruz, whom they have left, along with his family, in utter destitution.

They murdered Alejandro Mojica and Félix Santos; Mojica was killed in his own house and Santos was killed in a dry river bed. Both left wives and children. For fear of repression, they were buried on their own land. Isabel Cruz, Manuel Santos and Santos Urquilla were also taken away to an unknown destination.

A final tragedy occurred this week: yesterday afternoon, UCA (the University of Central America) was attacked for the first time and without any provocation. We want to express a special solidarity with the victims and the school. A full brigade from the national police started this operation at 1.15 p.m. They entered the campus shooting. One student who was found studying mathematics was murdered. His name was Manuel Orantes Guillén. I have also been told that various students have disappeared and that their families and the UCA are protesting at this invasion of an institution whose autonomy should be respected. What they have not done at the national university, no doubt because of fear, they have done at UCA, which is not armed to defend itself — a fact showing that it has been attacked without provocation. We hope to give more details of this, which is a serious offence against the civilised values and the rule of law in our country.

Let us think for a moment about the meaning of these months. Beloved brothers and sisters, I do not want to take more of your time, but it would be interesting now to analyse what these months have meant to a new government that started out with the intention of bringing us out of these horrific situations. And yet if what it aims for is to cut down the leaders of the people's organisation and impede the process which the people want, no other process can take place. Without roots among the people, no government can be effective, and it has no hope if it seeks to establish itself by blood and suffering.

I would like to make a special appeal to the men of the army, and specifically to the ranks of the National Guard, the police and the military. Brothers, you come from our own people. You are killing your own brother peasants when any human order to kill must be subordinate to the law of God which says, 'Thou shalt not kill'. No soldier is obliged to obey an order contrary to the law of God. No one has to obey an immoral law. It is high time you recovered your consciences and obeyed your consciences rather than a sinful order. The church, the defender of the rights of God, of the law of God, of human dignity, of the person, cannot remain silent before such an abomination. We want the government to face the fact that reforms are valueless if they are to be carried out at the cost of so much blood. In the name of God, in the name of this suffering people

31

whose cries rise to heaven more loudly each day, I implore you, I beg you, I order you in the name of God: stop the repression.

The church preaches your liberation just as we have studied it in the holy bible today. It is a liberation that has, above all else, respect for the dignity of the person, hope for humanity's common good, and the transcendence that looks before all to God and only from God derives its hope and its strength.

The Last Homily

24 March 1980
This was the last homily of Archbishop Romero, given at 5 p.m.
in the chapel at Divine Providence Hospital in San Salvador.

Through our various dealings with the publishing house of the newspaper *El Independiente,* I have been able to observe the filial sentiments of Doña Sara's children on the anniversary of their mother's death. Above all, I have seen the noble spirit that belonged to dear Doña Sara, who placed all her education and intelligence at the service of a cause that is so vital today: the true liberation of our people.

This afternoon, I believe that her brothers and sisters should not only pray for the eternal rest of their dear deceased one, but should especially heed her message, one that every Christian must live intensely. Many surprise us by thinking that Christianity should not meddle in these things, but our duty is the exact opposite.

You have just heard in the Lord's gospel that we must not love ourselves so much that we refrain from plunging into those risks history demands of us, and that those wanting to keep out of danger will lose their lives. On the other hand, those who surrender to the service of people through love of Christ will live like the grain of wheat that dies. It only apparently dies. If it were not to die, it would remain a solitary grain. The harvest comes because the grain of wheat dies. The earth allows itself to be sacrificed, broken; only in being broken does it produce the harvest.

I have chosen an excerpt from a Vatican II document that applies to dear Doña Sara now in heaven. It says this:

We know neither the moment of the consummation of the earth and of humanity nor the way the universe will be transformed. The form of this world, distorted by sin, is passing away and we are taught that God is preparing a new dwelling and a new earth in which righteousness dwells, whose happiness will fill and surpass all the desires of peace arising in human hearts. Then with death conquered God's children will be raised in Christ and what was sown in weakness and dishonour will put on the imperishable: charity and its works will remain and all of creation, which God made for human beings, will be set free from its bondage to decay.

We are warned that it is of no value to us to win the whole world if we lose ourselves. Nonetheless, the hope of a new earth should not weaken, but reinvigorate, our concern to perfect this earth, where the body of the new human family is already growing, a body which can be a foreshadowing of the new age. So, although we have to make a careful distinction between temporal progress and the growth of Christ's kingdom, temporal progress, insofar as it may contribute to a better ordering of human society, is still of great importance to the kingdom of God.

When we have spread human dignity, unity and freedom — in a word, all the excellent fruits of nature and our effort — throughout the earth in the spirit of the Lord and in accord with his command, we will find that, when Christ surrenders the eternal and universal kingdom to the Father, they will be free of all stain, illuminated and transformed. 'His kingdom will be a kingdom of truth and life, a kingdom of holiness and grace; a kingdom of justice, love and peace'. The kingdom is already mysteriously present on our earth; when the Lord comes its perfection will be completed.

This hope comforts us as Christians. We know that every effort to improve society, above all when society is so full of injustice and sin, is an effort that God blesses, that God wants, that God demands of us. And when one meets noble people like Doña Sarita, and sees her thinking embodied in little Jorge and in all those who work for these ideals, one must try to purify these ideals in Christianity, yes, to wrap them in hope for what is beyond. Our good deeds are stronger if done with faith. We have the security of knowing that what we plant on earth, if we nourish it with Christian hope, will never fail; we will find our efforts purified in that kingdom where merit lies in what we have done on this earth.

I believe that it would be vain to aspire to great visions of hope and struggle on this anniversary. We simply and gratefully remember this noble woman who understood the restlessness of her son and of all who work for a better world, who knew as well how to plant her share of wheat grain in the suffering of the people. There is no doubt that Doña Sara's self-giving is the guarantee that her reward is heaven, the reward that must come for making the sacrifice and showing the understanding that many need at this moment in El Salvador.

I implore all of you, beloved brothers and sisters, to look at these things in their historical context, to have hope, joined with a spirit of surrender and sacrifice. We must do what we can. All of us can do something. First, from the outset, we must have a sense of understanding. Maybe this blessed woman that we are remembering today could not do things directly, but she inspired those who could by understanding their struggle, and above all, by praying.

And even after her death, she lives on and says from eternity that it is worth the effort to work for the kingdom. If we illuminate with Christian hope those longings for justice, peace and goodness that we still have on this earth, they will be realised. Those who have put into their work a feeling of great faith, of love for God, of hope for humanity, find all that work now overflowing in the splendours of a crown. Such has been the reward for all of those who do that work, watering the earth with truth, justice, love and kindness. These deeds are not lost; purified by the spirit of God, their effects are our reward.

This holy mass, this eucharist, is clearly an act of faith. Our Christian faith shows us that in this moment contention is changed into the body of the Lord who offers himself for the redemption of the world. In the chalice, the wine is transformed into the blood that was the price of salvation. May this body broken and this blood shed for human beings encourage us to give our body and blood up to suffering and pain, as Christ did

35

— not for self, but to bring justice and peace to our people. Let us be intimately united, then, in faith and hope at this moment of prayer for dear Doña Sara and for ourselves.

At this point Archbishop Romero was shot.

Archbishop Romero: Martyr for Liberation

I came to know Archbishop Romero over a period of three years. I saw him first in Aguilares that night they killed Fr Rutilio Grande, SJ. The last time I spoke to him was a week before his martyrdom. I brought him a message of solidarity from the participants in the Fourth International Ecumenical Congress of Theology, which had just been held in São Paulo. It is with gratitude that I recall his friendship, the impact of his faith, and the inspiration he gave to theological reflection. Much has already been written about him and there will be more. This article seeks to be a first approximation to a theological analysis of his character and work in evangelical, ecclesial and social terms. Because it is analytical and not simply descriptive it attempts to reveal the roots of Archbishop Romero's character and work, and therefore it may also assist the church in its self-understanding and action, both in the archdiocese of San Salvador in the future and in similar situations in the Latin American continent.

1. The Gospel faith of Archbishop Romero

Archbishop Romero became without a doubt a quite exceptional figure both within the church and within society at large in Latin America. But so as to understand this, I want to begin by examining something deeper in him, something of which the social and ecclesial dimensions of his life were the expression, the vehicle. I want to plumb the ultimate mystery of every human being, that which is hidden in the depths of the heart, that source from which spring up both our daily lives and those actions we take at crucial moments. I want, in other words, to plumb that most simple yet most sublime thing we call faith.

Perhaps it appears to be saying little, or saying something very obvious, if I begin by describing Archbishop Romero as a man who believed in God. So little has the word 'God' come to mean it is easily taken for granted that we believe in him. On the other hand God can be so readily ignored that no longer does it seem to be rendering particular honour to his memory, or providing an adequate theological basis simply to say that he believed in God.

Yet for a Christian 'God' is a far from empty term. It is far from being an abstract, distant and ineffective reality. No, God is the source of all life, justice love and truth, and the ultimate horizon to which all these reach out. It is God who lays upon us the absolute demand that we live our lives in a way truly worthy of man, that we strive to make ourselves more human by ridding ourselves of what makes us less than human.

The first thing I want to say of Archbishop Romero, therefore, is that he had a profound faith in God. We know of the devotion, felt not feigned, with which he spoke of God in his homilies. We know of his solitary meditation and his simple, popular prayers. For him, to speak with God was something as straightforward and every-day as life itself.

And I also want to say of Archbishop Romero that he believed in God just as Jesus did. That is why I want to examine his following of Jesus from the precise stand-point of his faith. As with Jesus, to be in communion with God, to speak with God and to speak about God meant above all for Archbishop Romero making God's will real and effective. The measure of his faith can be gauged by the way he utterly and completely defended God's cause. Like Jesus he sought and found God's will as much in the minutiae of everyday life as in life's most profound and significant moments. He never made of God's will something trivial or routine as all of us Christians — bishops and priests as well — do only too often. We — and the church itself — lay down rules and regulations today just as in

38

the time of Jesus. We try to cut God down to size, to manipulate, even to empty him of meaning. Archbishop Romero placed no limits to God's will. On the contrary. He sought the will of God where it was in truth to be found: where the lives of men and women hang in the balance, where sin makes people into slaves, into human refuse, where there rises up a cry for justice, that hope for a society, and for man, which is growing in humanity. This is what we shall try to analyse in what follows.

1.1 Archbishop Romero believed in the God of the kingdom

His faith in God therefore made him a defender of life, and especially a defender of the lives of the poor. The anguish of the poor touches the very heart of God. That is why he saw in life, and in life at its most basic, the manifestation of God just as the prophet Isaiah had done before him. 'The world of food and work, of health and housing, the world of education — this is God's world. The world God wants is one in which "the workers will build houses and inhabit them, the peasants plant vineyards and eat their fruit" (Is 65:21). Poverty and desolation is a denial of God's will, a perverted creation in which God's glory is mocked and scorned. The fullness of the life to come is no palliative or consolation: faith in God begins with the defence of life here and now. The living man is God's glory. To be absolutely accurate, the living, poor man or woman is God's glory' (Lecture in the University of Louvain, 2 February 1980).

Because of his faith in God Archbishop Romero denounced our country's sin with a fierceness which can only be likened to that of the prophets of old, or to that of Bishop Bartolomé de las Casas, or to that of Jesus himself. Hardship, he declared, is not the natural destiny of the people of El Salvador. It is at root the outcome of unjust structures. With unequalled feeling he attacked the repression of people, the massacres, and the genocide.

He never ceased in his attack, he never tempered it, he never found prudent reasons for silence. Unlike others he never put the church's own security before the necessity of attacking repression. He had heard God saying 'Though you may multiply your prayers I shall not listen, for your hands are covered with blood' (Is 1:15).

'Sin' for him was really an offence against God because it is an offence against people. 'Sin' is indeed something which causes death — that is why it is mortal. One cannot see an offence against God: it becomes visible when one sees bloodstained corpses, when one hears the wailing of the mothers of those who have disappeared or been tortured. Since his faith was in the God of life, such sin was utterly counter to this faith. His faith bore him up in his denunciation of sin. It added to the harshness with which he exposed it. It enabled him to ignore the risks, both personal and institutional, that he had to run.

Through his faith in God Archbishop Romero worked and struggled towards a just solution to his country's problems. He believed in the God of the exodus who, today as yesterday, looks upon a captive and exploited people, hears their cries, then himself comes to free them, and to promise them a new land. But he also believed that this liberating will of God had to be made effective. He was not content, therefore, simply to speak in favour of life and to denounce all that destroyed it. Instead he placed himself clearly on the side of justice, that is to say on the side of the struggle to win a just way of life for the poor. He did not rely on purely political considerations but on his faith in God. That is why he did not stop where others hold back: at the struggle and at the organisation of the poor.

He was a man of peace. He was constantly on the side of peaceful solutions. But his faith brought him to accept the mystery of the conflict to which sin gives rise. He accepted that sin can only be overcome by a struggle against it. Like Mary he accepted calmly that God 'has pulled down princes from their thrones and exalted the lowly' (Lk 1:52). Some pharisaically see a source of scandal in the fact of historical conflict. For Archbishop Romero his acceptance of it was a demand made upon him by his faith in God.

And because he believed in a God who wills justice, Romero also embraced that other fact of life from which others hold themselves back, the fact that the poor have to liberate themselves, that they have to take charge of their own destiny, not simply be passive objects of benevolence 'from above'. He came to understand that in El Salvador 'above' means the gods of absolutised capitalism and national security and that the God

40

of liberation has to be met 'below'. It was because of that belief that Archbishop backed all just movements of the people which carried them towards freedom.

In this way Archbishop Romero believed in the God of the kingdom today in El Salvador just as Jesus had proclaimed it in his own day: a just society *for* men and women, and especially a just society *for* the poor. But he also believed that this new society for which battle had to be joined ought to be a society *of* new men and women, *of* men and women of the kingdom. He therefore never lost sight of the moral and spiritual dimensions of man. He encouraged the view that even in conflict and battle there arise true human values, those of solidarity, of generosity, of clarity of vision, the values, in a word, which Jesus proclaimed in the sermon on the mount. And therefore he was critical, as a pastor, of anything that might dehumanise people, even in their just struggles.

He was not guided in any way by political calculations, much less by thought of the popularity — or the notoriety — to which his constant preaching about the values of the people of the kingdom gave rise. He was guided by an unshakeable faith in a God who wills a new society — and who wills also a new kind of people. That is why, without waiting for the establishment of the new society, he insisted on the need here and now for purity of heart, magnanimity, dialogue and openness to conversion. He also spoke for those things which few today in El Salvador can mention without cynicism: forgiveness, and overcoming the instinct for vengeance.

No one who knew Archbishop Romero would see in these exhortations any ingenuousness, or the routine repetition of Christian verities. He would see rather a deep faith in God, a faith which pointed towards the utopia of the 'kingdom of God' and of 'the people of the kingdom'. He was well aware of the problems in the way of achieving both these utopias, but he never lost heart. He constantly proclaimed and promoted them because he believed in God's utopia and because he believed that such a utopia — even though it be never fully realisable — was the best way of bringing about man's greater humanity.

1.2 Archbishop Romero believed in the God of truth

Because of his faith in God Archbishop Romero associated his struggle for justice with the proclamation of the truth. No one spoke out as much and as clearly about the real situation in this country. Shortly before his martyrdom he was able to say, as, in his own day, Jesus too had said, that in more than two years of preaching no one had ever been able to accuse him of lying.

This love for, and constant preaching of, the truth had a profoundly humanising effect on the country. In the first place, it wasn't that Archbishop Romero merely told the truth: he told the whole truth. It sometimes happens, even if infrequently, that the truth is told. It is very rare indeed for the whole truth to be told, because this presupposes not only telling the truth but experiencing the demands that it makes on one. It implies bringing truth into the liberation struggle, but also making it a weapon in that struggle. It takes for granted that in the truth there is something which cannot be manipulated, that the effectiveness of the truth lies in its very telling. It is in this sense that Archbishop Romero was an impassioned teller of the truth.

Secondly, simply by speaking the truth Archbishop Romero restored value to the silenced, manipulated, distorted word. He made the word what it ought to be, the expression of reality. His Sunday sermons were listened to because in them the real situation in the country found its expression. In his preaching the daily hopes and griefs which the media usually either ignored or distorted found expression. No one in the country can any longer ignore the fact that the word, dialogue, speech have to be at the service of objective reality, not of partisan interests.

That love for the truth, that putting into words of the real state of affairs, was rooted in his faith in God. The phrase used by Christians at the end of the scripture readings, 'This is the word of the Lord', was not a commonplace for Archbishop Romero. It was an urgent commitment to go on preaching the word and using it to bring before people the real situation of the country. 'The word of God is not in chains', said St Paul. For Archbishop Romero it would have been a fearsome crime to have tied down, or to have ignored, that word both as it is to be found in scripture, and as it is to be found in the events of history. So he spoke, and spoke the truth. He believed that God is also the God of truth. He saw in the truths made manifest in history God's latest demands upon us, and a manifestation of

God in history.

1.3 Archbishop Romero believed in the God who makes things new

This faith in God meant that Archbishop Romero was not alarmed by historical change; rather, he made this change a vehicle of his faith. There were two main ways in which he demonstrated his faith in the newness God brings to pass. At a more strictly personal level he was able to grow, to change, even to undergo conversion. The beginning of his ministry in the Archdiocese coincided with the beginning of the persecution of the church and an increase in the repression of the people. He was changed by this new situation, he was converted. He was fifty-nine years old, an age at which people's psychological attitudes and mental patterns have usually already been formed. He was, moreover, at the summit of the church's institutional power structure, which like all power structures, tends towards establishment and immobility. Yet even from that position and at that age he demonstrated the true humanity of those who believe in God. He became someone new. He acquired a new and different sense of what it meant to be a Christian. He understood his ministry as a bishop in a new and different way.

As bishop he began a new form of pastoral activity. He even adopted a new theology, much to the surprise and alarm of those who preferred the old, the known, that with which they felt secure. He was constantly concerned with the new problems which the history of the church and of his country put before him. He did not choose which problems to respond to, knowing himself safest with the traditional ones. Quite the opposite: he faced up to new situations as they arose. To the very end he was concerned with what he called his apostolate of companionship to politically committed Christians, with the new situation in the country, and with the future — shown by his unceasing interest in events in Nicaragua. He was as much surprised as any one else by the changes which history brought. He was upset by his feeling of impotence, of being unable to produce a ready answer. But this did not paralyse him; it encouraged him to go on seeking the will of God in this new history.

This openness to new historical situations, this constant facing up to the challenge of the new, was simply the expression of his faith in a God whose mystery, as John says, is greater than our hearts, greater than any particular situation. Archbishop Romero readily accepted that God was also present in the old, certainly in his revelation in scripture and in the tradition of the church. That is why he was so scrupulously faithful to Vatican II, to Medellín and to Puebla. But the same conviction made him faithful to the Spirit of God, a Spirit which is not to be encapsulated in the traditions of the church but which blows when and where it wills. The when and the where have always to be sought out anew. There are no ready-prepared routes.

Because of his faith in the God who makes things new Archbishop Romero often had to journey alone, misunderstood by many of those around him, even by other bishops. He knew only that, like Abraham, he had to travel a road trusting in the Spirit of God. He knew that God is greater than the roads already travelled, greater than his own loneliness. He heard God's word 'Leave your country, your family and your father's house for the land which I will show you' (Gen 12:1). For Archbishop Romero, to believe in God meant taking that saying seriously, not reducing it to something manageable but letting God be ever the God of the new, following wheresoever the Spirit of God might lead.

1.4 Archbishop Romero believed in the God of the poor

Because of that faith Archbishop Romero found in the midst of the poor the pathway to belief in God. I am here speaking not so much of the good he did for the poor — I will examine that more closely later — but rather the good the poor did to him, as far as his faith was concerned.

In the first place he found *in* the poor the scandalous aspect of the mystery of God, as it is understood in Christianity. In the crucified of history the crucified God has made himself present. The kenotic dimension of God, God's emptying himself in other words, goes on being foolishness, a scandal. It is the dividing line between Christianity and other commonplace theistic beliefs. It is made manifest in the poor, in the oppressed and the repressed of his people. In their faces he saw the disfigured countenance of God.

And in the second place he encountered God *from the posi-*

tion of the poor. The problem of the locus of encounter with God presented itself to him as the problem of finding that place from which, afterwards, God might be found in any place. In hermeneutical theology that question is a matter of complex debate. Archbishop Romero resolved it very simply. His deep conviction can best be expressed in a neat sentence from the Puebla documents: 'Therefore — because they are poor — God comes to their defence and loves them' (n. 1142). This passage presupposes a relationship between 'God' and 'the poor', a preferential relationship within the overall relationship between 'God' and 'creation'. The beneficiaries of this partiality are those who, in their turn, can point out the locus of the right relationship with God.

For Archbishop Romero this did not mean idealising the poor. It meant that he had found the place from which an essential aspect of God could be known and from which it was possible to see in particular historical choices the criteria for the establishment of the kingdom, for the practical implications of truth, and the direction of change. It is taking a particular partial position in this way that makes it possible to transcend the apparent impartiality of finding God in any place and in any way, and therefore it was through his partiality for the poor that Archbishop Romero could be impartial and find God everywhere.

It is the Christian paradox that the mystery of the God who is always greater has been revealed primarily in what is small, what is less. It is from this lesser place that God has shown himself to be always greater. It is in this sense that it can be said that Archbishop Romero was evangelised by the poor. He was evangelised by the positive values he so often found in them, and they put him where he could correctly hear the Good News of God.

1.5 Archbishop Romero believed in the Father of Jesus, and bore witness to him like Jesus

In describing Archbishop Romero's faith, I have obviously been describing the Father of Jesus. The God of the kingdom, the God of truth, the God of the new, the God of the poor, these are names which describe Jesus' God. I would like, however, to bring this short analysis to a close by considering two features of

45

Jesus' attitude to his Father which Archbishop Romero also shared. Faith is a gift. But faith was not given to Archbishop Romero once and for all. Like Jesus he was exposed to temptation. He had to endure loneliness, ignorance, attack and persecution. He had to preserve his faith.

Faith was not given to him directly. Like Jesus he had to construct it all the time through ecclesial and historical action, which for him was the exercise of an archiepiscopal ministry and a leadership which was also a leadership within society, as we shall see in greater detail further on. Archbishop Romero not only had faith in God, he was also a faithful witness to the end. He became for many Christians what is said of Jesus in the Letter to the Hebrews — though of Jesus in all its fullness: 'He leads us in our faith and brings it to perfection' (12:2).

He believed in Jesus' God, and he believed like Jesus. This is the Gospel basis for his life and work, the basis of his impressive human qualities. I began this analysis of his character and work with his Gospel faith because that is the way that one can most readily come to understand his impact both as archbishop and as a leader in society. In fact it is impossible easily to distinguish between these two dimensions, between his personal faith and his ministerial action, because they are dialectically linked. His faith was the foundation for his actions, but in turn his actions made his faith concrete. There is no doubt that without understanding the gift of faith and the quality of his faith, it is impossible to have a full understanding of the quality of his action.

2. Archbishop Romero's archiepiscopal ministry

Archbishop Romero was not only a believer, a follower of Jesus. He was in addition an 'archbishop'. It seems to me to be very important indeed to insist that it was through his archiepiscopal ministry that his faith took concrete shape, and not despite his ministry, or on its fringe. There is no doubt that episcopacy is one of the most important aspects of the 'institution' of the church. Equally there is no doubt that the institutions of the church are going through a serious crisis precisely because of their incapacity to act as an adequate vehicle for a living faith.

Archbishop Romero knew how to bring faith and

episcopacy — the personal charism and the institutional — together. It was a remarkable gift, and an uncommon one, though he shared it with a considerable number of Latin American bishops of today. I want, in describing Archbishop Romero as a bishop, to do justice to his work. But indirectly this description might also contribute to the theology of episcopacy, something particularly necessary nowadays.

2.1 As archbishop, Mgr Romero confirmed the faith of his brethren

This duty, laid by Jesus on St Peter, Archbishop Romero carried out to perfection, and with surprising effect. The faith of the archdiocese has undoubtedly grown and deepened. The peasants and workers have made more profound their traditional, popular religion. The middle class, whose faith had been little more than conventional, or whose residual liberalism had driven them out of the church, has again begun to show its faith in the Gospel. At the level of the archdiocese's collective consciousness the faith has been given new strength. This is due in great measure to Archbishop Romero. He learned the lesson well that, as bishop, it was his duty to confirm the faith of his brethren. But he learnt it in a very particular way.

He came to realise that this basic ministry which he had to exercise as bishop is neither identical with, nor can be adequately carried out through, the teaching office. That is to say, it cannot be fulfilled simply by preserving, explaining and interpreting statements of the faith. He did not neglect the teaching office, as we shall see later. But he understood that faith is prior to the magisterium, that the *life* of faith precedes the formulations of faith. So in the ministry of confirming in the faith he saw something which was both deeper than, and prior to, the ministry of teaching: strengthening the brethren in that which is central to, which sums up, the faith: the following of Jesus.

It was the bishop's task, as he understood it, to make the Christian faith 'credible' at its deepest level. But he also understood that he should not do this in the first instance simply by using the full weight of his authority to proclaim the faith, or to demand it of others. He had to make the faith actual in himself. He had to progress in faith, remain loyal to it, live it out in particular situations, and accept the risks that follow from that.

The essential mark of the office of bishop is to be a 'witness' to the faith, truly and deeply. A bishop ought to be such that the faithful naturally believe that he believes, and so are themselves nourished and strengthened in their faith. What episcopacy adds to the witness to the faith borne by any Christian is the heavy responsibility of being a witness to the faith explicitly, and the power the position of a bishop gives to that witness.

2.2 As archbishop, Mgr Romero was the defender of the poor and the oppressed

It was not that he simply imitated Jesus as so many Christians do. No, he made this defence of the poor and oppressed a specific and a basic function of his episcopal ministry. His pastoral activity clearly put him on their side. He denounced the destitution from which they suffered, and its causes. He drew near to them. He defended their interests. At the administrative level he had the human and material resources of the archdiocese redistributed to their benefit.

In analysing his episcopate it is essential to realise that he made the defence of the poor his principal ministry. He thus restored something of great importance for the understanding of episcopacy which began at the time of the colonisation, but was afterwards lost. At the time of the colonisation the bishop was, *ex officio*, the 'protector of the Indians'. On the assumption, all too correct, that the Indians were going to be marginalised, exploited and annihilated, the bishop had the task of protecting them, defending them from exploitation by either the military or the colonists.

This deeply Christian and ecclesial insight into the role of a bishop, which goes back four centuries, was revived in our day by Archbishop Romero. The poor, the oppressed, any one in need knew this, and turned to him for help. They came to the Archbishop whether they wanted injustices denounced, their rights, or missing people found. They came to him to mediate when lands had been seized or when the security forces had surrounded churches. It was not that they simply came to him as a friend, seeking consolation. They came to him as a protector who was in duty bound to put the full weight of his episcopal authority at the service of the poor and the oppressed.

If the poor came to him spontaneously it was because he had himself created that model of a bishop. In doing so he achieved something of the greatest importance — though it may seem, when put down on paper, a little ambiguous. What he succeeded in doing was 'institutionalising' the preferential option for the poor. To 'institutionalise', here, does not mean to bureaucratise or trivialise. On the contrary, it means that not only Christians as individuals should make this option for the poor but also the church as such, as an institution, should opt for them, and should also place its institutional resources at their service.

Precisely because he was the archbishop and therefore the foremost representative of the institutional church, Archbishop Romero made it possible to speak of the church of the poor. And, because of him the people did judge the various ecclesiastical institutions by this criterion, by their defence of the poor and the oppressed.

2.3 As archbishop, Mgr Romero evangelised the totality of the country

He carried out Jesus' command to his apostles to make disciples of 'all'. He was aware that as archbishop, he was responsible for making evangelisation 'total', that it was his duty to evangelise 'totalities', human, social and historical.

Because both archdiocese and country are small, and their problems similar, the task of evangelising the 'totality' was made easier. In a small country the archdiocese was important. The archbishop's prestige, and his use of the media, meant that he could reach out into every corner of the land. It was relatively simple for him to evangelise the whole of El Salvador. For Archbishop Romero this implied three important things:

1. Evangelising the totality means first evangelising everyone, trying to proclaim the good news to all, whatever their personal or social situation. However, Archbishop Romero knew very well that the totality of human beings is divided into different groups by pastoral criteria, let alone social and economic ones. Accordingly he tried to evangelise all, but in different ways, not simply in the techniques he used but also in the purpose and direction of evangelisation. He developed a popular pastoral

strategy which took account of the need for an increase in popular religion, a strategy of 'companionship' for those Christians most involved in organisations and political parties and a strategy aimed at conversion for Christians who were part of the structures of economic and political power.

2. Evangelising the totality also means evangelising the structural reality of the country, that is, the totality of the country understood not now as the sum of the individuals in it but as the structures which shape the lives of those individuals. In this sense Archbishop Romero evangelised constantly, denouncing unjust structures, proclaiming the social, economic and political changes required and promoting the particular programmes which seemed most likely to lead to that structural change. Archbishop Romero saw clearly that at the present time the church has to combine 'evangelising *all* people' with 'evangelising the country in *all* its aspects, social, economic and political'.

3. To evangelise a totality also means adequately to understand the ecclesial function of small ecclesial groups, while avoiding the temptation of reducing the church to them. Clearly, because of the inherently elaborate structure of the church small groups will constantly spring up, whether in the traditional forms of religious congregations, or in the form of lay movements, or in the rather more modern form of basic Christian communities. Now is not the time to pass judgement on these groups, which, of their very nature, have to be kept quite small. I want rather to think of them in relation to the totality of evangelisation. I want to talk about the two theoretical models of basic Christian communities.

According to one possible model, the church should promote these groups, take refuge in them, use them as the last stronghold of the faith where the needs, human and Christian, of a very small number of individuals can be satisfied. This model implies a reduction of evangelisation and, at root, a defeatism about the church: the aim is to save all that can be saved of the church.

According to the second model, the Christian groups are the inevitable result of mass evangelisation. Basic communities arise out of an awareness of the country's problems and of the need to establish the kingdom of God. They arise in response to this need, and as a means of fulfilling it. So this model is not so much one of 'reduction' as of 'concentration'. The church concentrates on these groups. It does this not so that it may better attend to the needs of a few, but so as to be a better leaven to all, and has this intention quite explicitly.

Ultimately the fundamental difference between the two models is that, according to the first, the church carries on being turned in on itself, and in the second it is at the service of the kingdom. In fact, of course, neither model exists in its pure form. I want simply to draw attention to the fact that precisely because Archbishop Romero wanted to evangelise the totality he encouraged the second, rather than the first, of the two models of basic communities — which in his view applied equally to lay movements and religious congregations. In his heart of hearts he believed that the evangelisation of the few, and a form of Christian life which could only serve the needs of a few, profoundly contradicted the word of God addressed to all, and put in doubt the efficacy of that word.

2.4 In his evangelisation, Archbishop Romero dealt in totalities

I mean by this that he understood evangelisation to be something which ought to be expressed through the totality of the church, both in its this-wordly and in its transcendental aspects, in personal and in social terms, in the church's liturgical and educational life, and so on. To the totality of the object of evangelisation, as we have described it above, the church had to respond with its own totality.

Archbishop Romero himself did not particularly develop a theory of evangelisation. He was inspired rather by Paul VI's encyclical *Evangelii Nuntiandi,* which he applied to the situation of El Salvador and filled out in some respects. He lived it out in his own apostolate and he insisted that all the pastoral workers of the Archdiocese should also implement it.

1. Archbishop Romero attached the highest importance to the explicit proclamation of the word. Both through his own Christian conviction and through his personal charism as a preacher he made the word his most important instrument of evangelisation. He proclaimed the word as the word of God, and in his homilies spent a long time explaining it. But it is important to add that he believed the word of God was still manifesting itself

in the events of contemporary history in 'the signs of the times'. Moreover he believed that the very proclamation of the word had its own efficacy. It is not only a proclamation about truths, it is truth itself. And that is why it is effective: because it makes present that which it proclaims. It was for these reasons that he so profoundly believed in the proclamation of the word as a means of evangelisation.

2. Archbishop Romero attached the highest importance to making the word come true, to turning the good news into a good reality. In the third part of this essay we will see how he turned this proclamation of the word into a force for the transformation of society. What I want to stress here is that he did not reduce making the word come true simply to the ethical level, secondary to an evangelisation already carried out in proclamation: he insisted that implementation is an essential part of evangelisation. Hence his insistence that full liberation was part of evangelisation. Indeed, his preaching embodied a dialectic between the 'proclamation' and the 'realisation' of the good news, each of which threw light on the other.

3. Archbishop Romero also attached the highest importance to the witness of life as a means of evangelisation: that is to say, the holiness of the preacher was all-important. Just as he believed in the kingdom of God and the man of the kingdom, so it was his deep conviction that the efficacy of preaching was inseparable from the credibility of the preacher. His most valuable contribution here was to pin down the centrality of holiness. A preacher certainly ought to possess the Christian virtues, the marks of a follower of Jesus. But as a preacher he ought to give a yet more fundamental witness: he must not abandon his people, he must travel along with them and be ready, like the good shepherd, to give even his life for them.

4. These three aspects of evangelisation are to be found in *Evangelii Nuntiandi*. Archbishop Romero emphasised a fourth element: that of prophetic denunciation. He was renowned in this regard both for his unequalled courage and for his solid incorruptibility. It is important to stress once again that he even saw this denunciation as good news, a sort of Gospel *sub specie contrarii*. It was a sort of proclamation of good through the rejection of evil. Archbishop Romero accordingly always denounced objective sin with great severity, but he always main-

tained the accent of good news when speaking to the oppressors. They, too, were his brothers, of whom God requires conversion and for whom, once converted, there is good news.

For their part the powerful, the oligarchy, big capital, reacted violently against him. As they had once said of Jesus, they said that Archbishop Romero was mad, that he was a new Beelzebub, that he was a political agitator trying to stir up the masses. Money was poured out to belittle and calumniate him. Rarely can there have been so irrational and violent a campaign against a prophet. But Archbishop Romero saw it all as part of the price a true prophet has to pay. He took it as evidence that what he stood for was the truth. But equally he saw in those who mounted the campaign people to whom the Gospel was also addressed. Like Jesus, he warned them of the dangers of their unjust wealth. As he so vividly put it: 'pull the rings off your fingers before they cut off your hands'. Like Jesus he strove always to hold out to them the promise of true happiness, such as was given to Zacchaeus after his conversion: 'Today a blessing has come upon this house'.

5. For Archbishop Romero the symbol of his 'total' evangelisation was the cathedral, 'his' cathedral. He had no property of his own, as his will demonstrated, but the cathedral was especially dear to him. He saw in it a symbol of the church and of the country, in all their nobility and in all their tragedy. He made the cathedral his 'cathedra' *par excellence*, the place to which the people were summoned, the place which gave unity to hundreds of priests and nuns, the place from which his message went out to the nation and the world. But the cathedral was also the place where the people were massacred, the place where they sought sanctuary. It was a hospital for the wounded, the scene of the funerals of the dead of the church and of the people. Several times the cathedral was seized by popular organisations, several times opened up and closed down. It was the scene of liturgies and hunger strikes.

This cathedral, just as it was, a symbol of sorrow and of hope, a meeting place for the church and for the people, Archbishop Romero made his own. From it he preached the truth. In the presence of the bodies of the dead he kept alive the hope of the people. He wanted the cathedral to be what it ought above all to be: the constant source of the proclamation of the good news, the Gospel. This man who was by nature rather shy was genuinely transfigured in the cathedral. In it he became aware that the Gospel was for all Salvadoreans, for the whole country. He made the cathedral the centre both of the church and of the nation. It will never be possible to write the history of the church or of the nation without telling the story of Archbishop Romero's cathedral.

2.5 Archbishop Romero carried out the teaching office of a bishop

It is obvious that, at the present time, this particular aspect of the episcopal ministry has its problems. People are not as ready as they were to accept the magisterium. But it is also obvious, and especially in Latin America, that many episcopal documents have been produced which are truly inspirational, and which are giving a new vigour to the teaching office. As a teacher of the truth, Archbishop Romero was one of those bishops who helped bring this about. He was well aware of the grave responsibility involved in teaching, he was aware both of the difficulty of, and the need for, this role, and of the need, even for a bishop, of 'learning to teach'. The following were the most innovative and most remarkable aspects of his work as a teacher:

1. He was able to link the church's general teaching — whether it was at the Latin American level (Medellín and Puebla) or at the world-wide level (Vatican II and papal encyclicals) — to the situation in the country. He demonstrated this ability both in his four pastoral letters, which were on the whole doctrinal, as well as in his Sunday sermons, which were more catechetical in style. He was able to achieve this, not through an *a priori* fidelity to the church's documents but because he looked for, and found, the enduring truths expressed in them. He understood that in what others have taught in the past there is truth to be found — though obviously to different degrees — and that there is still a demand for the truth today. Relating the church's teaching to conditions in El Salvador did not therefore mean simply applying universally applicable documents to particular situations, but looking to see what light truth already expressed might shed upon that truth which is being sought in the new situation. The reason that that light could be found in existing documents was

54

precisely that it was being looked for in a particular situation.
tion.

2. Archbishop Romero was aware of the demands made upon
him by truth. In other words, he did not choose the problems
with which he had to deal: he tackled those which history put
before him, however novel and difficult they might be. He
taught what was worth teaching because it was required by a
real situation, even though there might be no ready-made and
safe doctrine on the matter. Truth was not the only aim of his
magisterium: another was relevance. And it is because his
pastoral letters do not simply contain general truths but are also
relevant that they have been widely distributed, and even
translated into other languages.

3. Even in fulfilling his office of teacher, Archbishop Romero
was quite consciously pastoral in approach. This was reflected
in the manner of his teaching, in his firmness and in his humility. He was firm when he was clear on an issue, he was humble
when the solution to a new problem was, by its very nature, pro-
visional: more a search for, than a possession of, the truth. So,
for example, he put forward his pastoral letter on popular
organisation as the first step towards a dialogue which, in the
nature of the case, had to be continued.

He taught with episcopal authority, but not with episcopal
exclusivity. Thus, without shirking ultimate responsibility, he
was in continual consultation with experts in the social sciences,
with theologians, with analysts of the national situation and its
developments. Above all, he took account of the people. He
tried to answer the real questions which ordinary Christians asked, and took their opinions into consideration when he replied.
One example is the questionnaire he sent round the basic communities in the archdiocese before setting off for Puebla.

And finally, he taught to the extent that he went on learning. He gave the impression of putting forward a truth which
was, of its very nature, always open to further refinement, and
even to change, which of its very nature required a constant process of learning. The constant refinement of his teaching was the
consequence not only of development in the realm of theory —
though that certainly played its part — but also of constant contact with the real life of church and society. Archbishop
Romero learned from real life and learned from it in a Christian

way because he truly believed in a God who goes on revealing himself in history. That is why he taught in the measure that he learned. It is no paradox to say that Archbishop Romero taught to the extent that he was taught by the world about him. He united in himself the heavy responsibility of teaching with the equally heavy responsibility of learning, and in doing so he exemplified something which is of the greatest importance for the office of bishop.

2.6 As archbishop, Mgr Romero was head of the body of the archdiocese

In saying that I want to insist that the archdiocese could not be understood without him — but then neither could he be understood outside the context of the archdiocese. At the theoretical level, the ecclesial reality of the archdiocese has to be thought of as a body, with the archbishop at the head. This became a reality under Archbishop Romero.

1. The figure of Archbishop Romero cannot be understood outside the context of the archdiocese. As he himself confessed, right at the beginning of his archiepiscopal ministry he was confronted by the very best that the archdiocese could offer. The martyrdom of Fr Grande, the support of the majority of the clergy and, above all, contact with the sufferings of the people — all these changed him. Over three long years of persecution the courage of the Christians, their sufferings and their faith moulded the archbishop himself. It is in this sense one can say of Archbishop Romero that he was indeed a symbol, an expression of the highest Christian reality of the archdiocese. Even though he brought with him to the office those human and Christian qualities which have already been described, in a very real sense the Christian community made the archbishop.

2. This relationship, real and not just administrative, between the archbishop and the archdiocese, explains two very important facts, the unification of the church, and the creation of a 'body' of evangelists. Archbishop Romero brought about a unity within the church in the archdiocese. Never before had there been such a common sense of purpose among the priests, the religious and the pastoral workers. This unity was not idealistic. There was a right-wing minority among the pastoral workers who were in opposition to the archbishop. There were also those

who wanted to go further than Archbishop Romero in involving the church in social and political life. Towards both groups he was understanding, but firm. Those on the right almost entirely abandoned him; with those on the left he kept up a dialogue right to the end, listening to them and learning from them.

3. The important thing about this unification is that it was productive. Archbishop Romero tried to make even the inevitable tensions sources of growth. The archdiocese united round a mission, the work of evangelisation we have described, and not just round church affairs. And in addition suffering and persecution cemented the unity.

Yet even this mission gave rise to disunity, not so much within the archdiocese as with other bishops in the country, with some priests and with Christians belonging to the ruling classes. To give Archbishop Romero his due, it was not he who cut himself off from them, but they who cut themselves off from him. The origin of the breach was not his personality — he was always kindness and humility itself — but the church which he inspired. The division among the bishops especially, caused him great pain and worry because of the scandal it gave to the faithful. It impoverished the church's mission in the country; it gave support to those who criticised the church of the archdiocese. But he put fidelity to his apostolate to the poor, as he saw it before God, before the pain of disunion.

4. This genuine unification of the archdiocese found expression in an immense power to gather the church together. This was certainly demonstrated when Archbishop Romero said mass, but it was also evident in all sorts of church activities. The unity was a real source of strength to the pastoral workers. Archbishop Romero succeeded in creating a 'pastoral body' made up of priests, nuns, catechists, delegates of the word and so on. As a 'body', its strength was more than the sum of its parts. The people understood that the whole of the archdiocese, and Archbishop Romero himself, was behind every one of the church's activities.

It is in this sense, a sense which is historical and effective not simply legal or abstract, that we can say Archbishop Romero was the head of the archdiocese. He lived by what was best and most Christian among the people, so that they saw him as their real representative, their real symbol. In a profound sense Archbishop Romero let himself be made a bishop by his people, and the people were grateful to him for making them truly the body of the church.

2.7 As archbishop, Mgr Romero changed the meaning of the institutional power of the church

It is clear that, in Latin America at least, the church as an institution still has great power in society. This power can be understood in many different ways. One extreme is the use of politico-ecclesiastical means to influence society or impose rules from above; the other is for the church to reduce itself to an inward-looking community which abandons the world to its fate or seeks to change it merely by a subjective witness of holiness.

Archbishop Romero exercised an 'institutional' power, but one which was different from both those types. Without seeking to do so, he became an important social leader in the country, a mediator, and sometimes an arbiter, in a great variety of conflicts within society. Groups of very different tendencies turned to him for help. It is important to examine what Archbishop Romero thought about this power and its origin, given that he did not reject it. It is important to see how he reconciled the 'institutional' power with the power at the 'service' of the poor, the majority of the population.

1. Archbishop Romero certainly did not understand the institutional power of the church in terms of the first model. The institutional power of the church cannot be regarded as analogous to the power of the state in such a way as to make the state the church's 'natural' partner, leaving the people as no more than the object of these two powers above them. In this model, which is basically the old model of 'Christendom', the ideal for the church as an institution is to be on good terms with the state, avoid conflicts with it or to resolve them, when they arise, at the expense of the people.

Archbishop Romero destroyed this formal model by his practice. The people, in his view, were not only not just the objects of the state's benevolence; they were not the objects of any benevolence. Power from above, therefore, is not power, not even power for the benefit of the people. Accordingly the church could not reproduce this model, all the more since its supposed natural partner, the state, had directly persecuted it.

It was because of this that Archbishop Romero made various gestures to destroy the image of the power of the institutional church as analogous to that of the state. That is why, for example, he took part in no ceremony, political or ecclesiastical, which presented the two powers as being on the same footing, and existing in supposed harmony. That is why he vividly said that it was not the church but the people which had problems with the state, and that is why the church clashed with the state. He wanted to make it clear that one cannot think of the institutional power of the church as power 'from above' like the state's power, or of the state as the church's natural partner.
2. But neither did he think of the church as a purely spiritual community, one far removed from any sort of social power. What he really did was to change the notion of power. The institutional power of the church ought to be exercised through those means which are proper to the church, especially through the word which creates a common awareness, and not through politico-ecclesiastical means, in a search for concessions from the state. It ought to be exercised for the good of the people, and not for the good of the church as an institution.

Archbishop Romero did not achieve this change in the understanding of power simply by intellectual development but by changing the church's base. The church found its place, its home, among the people. It was from the people that it learnt what it was to place its power at the service of the people. It is a commonplace that power in the church should be 'service', but Archbishop Romero made it a reality by placing the church among those whom it was its duty to serve. The institutional power of the church was exercised now, not just for the people, but also with the people, not from above but from below.

2.8 Our description of Archbishop Romero's episcopal ministry has done no more than translate into modern terms — as Puebla asked (682-84) — the gospel portrait of the pastor, of Jesus. With him, the sheep were safe (Jn 10:9); his function was to give them life, and life in abundance (Jn 10:10); he knew his sheep, and his sheep knew him (Jn 10:14); he was always ready to lay down his life for his sheep (Jn 10:11)

It is beyond doubt that Archbishop Romero's Gospel faith helped him to make his episcopal ministry Christian. But it is also beyond doubt that his position as bishop helped him to give his faith substance and surprising efficacy. Whatever the theories about the episcopate, Archbishop Romero demonstrated by his actions that it is possible to carry out this ministry in a Christian way. He also demonstrated how important the position of bishop can be in making the faith effective in Latin America. Archbishop Romero did not theorise about all the various issues currently being debated in the theology of the episcopate. By his ministry he brought into being a new theology of the episcopate which does not ignore its traditional characteristics but gives them form and substance for a new historical situation. Speaking purely sociologically, one cannot expect to find many people with the archbishop's human, Christian qualities. But speaking theologically we have in him a model of what a bishop, with a Gospel faith, ought nowadays to be like, and an example of how important it is to be a bishop to make that faith effective for liberation. That is no small merit of Archbishop Romero's.

3. Archbishop Romero's judgement on the country

Archbishop Romero truly loved his country. In his apostolate as archbishop he put that love into action. Without wanting to do so, he became a true leader. His main influence in the country was in the religious sphere, but, as he was well aware, that was immediately translated into a direct social influence, and into an indirect political one — though in no way did he directly involve himself in politics. One can represent what he did in the social field by the following scheme: Archbishop Romero constantly denounced all that disgraced the country; he proclaimed tirelessly the sort of new society we need; he strove to humanise the processes of change. To record all the positions he took up, all the work that he did during his three years of office would be an endless task. Instead I am going to attempt to analyse the Christian principles which lay behind his judgement on the country, and to go on from that to examine his actual judgement on the three programmes which are currently before the country.

3.1 The Christian principles

In speaking of these I mean, in the first place, the general principles today ordinarily accepted in the church which arose out of Medellín, though they have not been effectively accepted in conservative circles, even as general principles.

3.1.1 In my view four fundamental principles guided Archbishop Romero's judgement.
1. The church is not the same thing as the kingdom of God. It is rather the servant of the kingdom. It ought, therefore, to practise that love and that justice which make possible particular historical expressions of the kingdom. it ought to be an instrument at the service of the kingdom and in consequence cooperate with those who truly want a more just society, even if they are not explicitly Christians.
2. The poor are those for whom the kingdom is primarily intended. Not that the kingdom should simply be constructed for them: they themselves should be the makers of their own destiny. It follows that they cannot be denied a substantial involvement in any process leading to the establishment of the kingdom.
3. As the servant of the kingdom the church ought also to promote the values of people of the kingdom, both while the new society is being built and when it is at length achieved.
4. For the church in any way to impede, obstruct or to destroy either the kingdom of God or the people of the kingdom is sinful. This sin covers both the personal and the structural level; it inevitably has degrees of gravity, and awareness of these will be important when making judgements about actual situations and developments.

3.1.2 These principles were very much at work in all that Archbishop Romero did, but he was also well aware that, because they are 'general' principles they have to be given historical form in accordance with the signs of the times. The need to give the principles historical form was an important part of his understanding of them. He therefore gave new importance to the much-neglected area of pneumatology — that is to say, to the affirmation that the Spirit is constantly at work in history as it changes.

In order to understand the actual judgements which Archbishop Romero made about the country one has to bear in mind the historical application he gave to some key principles. Of these the most important in my view were the following:

1. Archbishop Romero gave historical identity to the reality of 'the poor'. He went beyond the purely spiritual idea of poverty — though he recognised the profound truth this Gospel formulation contains — and described its characteristic features in El Salvador, as Puebla did (nn 31-39). But more than that, he saw the poor not just as isolated individuals but as the 'masses' of the country. To speak of the poor was to speak of 'the' problem in El Salvador. He regarded this great mass not just as a sum of individuals but as a collectivity, as a people — however much sociologically one has to nuance this statement. He saw in this collectivity a social grouping opposed to the ruling group — though as a pastor he was not concerned to analyse the class nature of those groups. In this way he advanced beyond the usual view of a poor person as a peaceable individual who is, at most, the source of an ethical demand upon us, to a view of the poor as a collectivity, the very existence of which — and increasingly so as it grows in self-understanding — is the sign of social conflict.

2. Archbishop Romero translated into practical terms the idea that the people ought to be the makers of their own destiny, and not simply the objects of real or supposed charity. Hence he understood the logic of moving from 'people' to 'organised people'. In this sense he defended as a Christian principle the right and need of people to organise. Though as a pastor he imposed on no one the obligation of joining an organisation, he positively encouraged them to do so, though without going so far as to point out which particular organisation came closest to fulfilling the ideal of the organised people.

He also grew in understanding of the purposes of organising the people. From the very beginning he saw the legitimacy of people organising themselves to defend legitimate rights or to fight for demands. But he also came to understand, and especially in the last months of his life, the importance of the people organising so as to gain political power in some form or be substantially represented in political power. He recognised that no political programme will successfully benefit the majority of the people unless the people's own organisations play a major part in the political life of the country.

3. In his promotion of a more just society he introduced the novel idea of the 'viability' of theory and of practice. The problem of the viability of theory led him to study and analyse which of the different political programmes would best ensure that the new society resembled the kingdom of God. The viability of practice concerned him as a pastor. It was as a pastor and not as a political analyst that he indicated those courses of action which, in his view, were most likely to bring the new society into being. Naturally, there is a tension between the viability of theory and the viability of practice, and Archbishop Romero understood this. But it is important to emphasise once again that in making the kingdom of God an historical reality he did not limit himself to proclaiming it, but thought hard about the viable ways of building the kingdom in this country.

3.1.3 In the process of giving Christian principles historical application, Archbishop Romero constantly deepened them, and at times he even changed his mind. His pastoral letters and his Sunday homilies are the history of this historicalisation. However, it is important to stress that this process of application, with all its complexity and nuances, even with its changes, went in a definitei, historical direction. This has to be said because, and especially since his death, he has frequently been presented as someone who was a defender of human rights in the abstract, who loved peace and justice, but who lacked any clear, practical, historical commitment. It is true that because he touched on a whole variety of different issues, and did so in such changing circumstances one can always find a quotation which can be exploited. It is possible to contrast things he said on different occasions in such a way as to suggest that, having said everything, in the end Archbishop Romero had said nothing. But that was never his intention, nor is it an objective picture of what he did.

Archbishop Romero did not adapt his general Christian principles to his own time simply on the basis of abstract theological reasoning or the evolving magisterium of the church about socio-political matters, though he made use of both. The principle which lay behind this process of adaptation was the actual history of his country or, to put it theologically, the manifestation of the Spirit in that history. That is why his judgements became increasingly specific as he himself progressed in discovering the will of God for the country in specific cases.

And as a way of checking on the validity of the development and the direction of his social thinking one ought not to ignore the reaction, both at home and abroad, to his active involvement: the public 'image' which the people as a whole and different social groups had of him. That reaction, that image, are proof enough that his actions had a definite direction, that his commitment was not merely to the universal values of peace, love, justice and human rights but to the programmes which would best guarantee those values.

3.2 Judgement on the three political programmes

On the basis of the criteria already cited, their historical application and development, Archbishop Romero passed judgement on the three programmes before the country. He called them the programme of the oligarchy, the programme of the governing junta, and the popular programme.

3.2.1 He condemned the policy of the oligarchy because it was clearly sinful. 'All in all, the right stands for social injustice. There is no justification for maintaining a right-wing stance', he told *El Diario de Caracas* (19 March, 1980). His fourth pastoral letter denounced the programme as idolatrous, that is to say based upon a lie. It was an idol, moreover, which, in order to survive, necessarily needed victims. This programme is not viable on Christian principles, nor, in Archbishop Romero's view, was it viable historically since the people, after fifty years of misery and with their present level of political awareness, could tolerate it no longer.

3.2.2 His judgement of the policy of the governing junta changed between the first and the second junta. He was hopeful about the first one. He did not give the coup of 15 October his blessing, nor did he give it unconditional support — though he gave it critical support. He saw that there was the chance of achieving the Christian principles outlined above. There were grounds for hope in the fact that the coup had been bloodless, in the honesty and the intentions of many of the new rulers, in the promises of radical reform and of dialogue with the popular organisations. But neither did this programme become viable. Repression continued. There was no information about the fate of all those who had vanished for political reasons. Those who were responsible were not brought to trial — something which Archbishop Romero regarded as a requirement of simple justice and as a sign that there had been a break with the past. The reforms could not be carried out. The resignations of all the honourable members of the government convinced him that the programme would not work.

The second junta had a clearer political programme. Archbishop Romero defined it as 'reforms with the garrote', reforms accompanied by repression. With increased vigour he condemned, as he had always done, the repression of the people. This had become enormously worse both in terms of the number of people involved, and of the degree of cruelty with which it was carried out. He condemned the final aim of the repression, the destruction of the popular organisations. It was the aim of that part of the government which, Archbishop Romero said, acted like a parallel government. He was brought to the point where, with unequalled passion, he called upon the soldiers and other members of the security forces not to obey unjust orders to kill. These were the last words of his last sermon:

> In the name of God, then, and in the name of this suffering people whose cries rise more loudly to heaven each day, I plead with you, I beg you, I order you in the name of God: stop the repression! (23 March 1980.)

This repression made the announced agrarian reform suspect. Though he stressed its necessity he foresaw its impossibility because, as scripture says, land stained with blood will not bear fruit (cf. Genesis 4:12). Agrarian reform ought not to be thought of as a gift to the people. It is something they have earned by the blood which they have shed. Even in the days of the first junta Archbishop Romero laid down the real popular significance which agrarian reform ought to have but which he did not see when it first began to be implemented in March. As he said:

> Agrarian reform should not be undertaken simply so as to find a way of salvaging the capitalist economic system, and allowing it to go on developing in such a way that wealth is

accumulated and concentrated in the hands of a few, whether they be of the industrial, commercial or banking sectors of society. Nor should it be a way of quietening down the peasants, to prevent them going on organising and increasing their political, economic and social involvement. Agrarian reform ought not to make the peasants dependent upon the state. It ought to leave them free in their relationship with the state (Sermon of 16 December 1979).

He drew the consequences of his denunciation of this political programme. He asked the Christian Democrats to re-think their position in the government. Just five days before his death he gave the following answer to a journalist who was questioning him about this:

I am no expert in politics. I can only repeat what I have heard from prominent analysts. Even though it is true they have the good intention of carrying through structural reforms, the Christian Democrats run a grave risk in being part of a government which is engaged in such fearful repression. In this way the Christian Democrat Party is becoming an accomplice in the destruction of the people. I want to tell this to you journalists, you who should be so clear and objective in your reporting of what is going on in El Salvador. I have often heard it said by people who live abroad and do not understand what is going on here, 'the Christian Democrats are there. They are carrying out reforms. What more do you want? Why do you complain?' So it should be made clear that though we have the Christian Democrat Party, we have reforms, the only thing the people get out of it is terrible repression (Interview with *El Diario de Caracas,* 19 March 1980).

It is in this context that one has to understand his letter to President Carter. The United States has no right to intervene in this country, no right to lend support to a policy which is said to be opposed to the oligarchy but which is, in reality opposed to the interests of the people, no right to provide military support just as the repression grows in intensity (cf. his sermon of 17 February 1980).

Archbishop Romero had no objections to a reformist policy in itself, provided it opened the way to reforms, and to the integration of the people and their organisations into the political process. But he did not regard this superficially reformist policy as one which was viable for Christians. Nor did he believe that the people would support it in the long term.

3.2.3 Over the three-year period his judgement about the popular programme evolved to the point where, in the last three months of his life, he came to think of it as the one which offered most hope for the country. He thought this for two reasons: the others would not work, and the popular organisations, which were the main champions of the popular programme, had gradually matured.

We have already described how the task of giving historical identity to the reality of poverty and the need for the poor to be the 'makers of their own destiny' had brought the archbishop face to face with the situation of the popular organisations. He devoted a large part of his third and fourth pastoral letters to this topic. I want now briefly to sum up his attitude towards the popular organisations, what he criticised in them, what the criticism meant, his support for them and the hopes that they engendered in him. For though the general tendency of his attitude was clear, it was complex and nuanced.

Archbishop Romero criticised all he saw as wrong-headed or dangerous in the popular organisations, both from a Christian and from an ordinary human point of view. He criticised all that he regarded as dehumanising in them, either in their effect on their members or in their effect on the country. He warned them severely against the danger of thinking that the point of view of their own organisation was the only possible one, and against the danger of reducing everything to politics and neglecting other areas of life. He accused them several times of being dogmatic and sectarian, of being divided among themselves, of being separated from other political groups and even from the people themselves. He denounced some of their disproportionately violent actions. On occasion he even denounced violence which turned into terrorism — though this he did not regard as typical of the popular organisations so much as of the politico-military groups. He accused them of claiming to be more representative of the people than they actually were, of sometimes failing to take account of the religious feelings of the people and their most cherished expressions of this feeling. In some extreme cases, he said, they wanted to manipulate or even to destroy the people's Christian faith. There were periods, and especially during the first junta, when he was deeply hurt by criticisms made of him, and by some signs of disloyalty.

It is important, however, to make clear what this criticism meant. His love for the truth moved him to denounce whatever he saw to be mistaken, though he perfectly well understood that so vast a social phenomenon as the popular organisations would be bound to make some mistakes. His criticism of them was different from his criticism of the other two programmes. He criticised the popular organisations because he had hopes for them. He wanted them to improve, to grow and to serve the people better. He denounced the absolutisation of politics because 'it could encourage a lack of effective interest in other real problems or a failure to take account of the ideological criteria of the rank and file' (4th Pastoral Letter, n 49). He attacked sectarianism because 'it changes what could be a force for the people's good into an obstacle, to their interests and to radical social change' (*ibid.*). He denounced slights against the Christian faith because they showed no respect for the reality of the faith among the people and because it 'would be a mistake to place in opposition to each other the energies of the organisations and the energies of the church' (*ibid.* n 66).

On the other hand, in the popular organisations Archbishop Romero saw a range of humane, Christian values which were beneficial for the country as a whole and from which the church would do well to learn. He admired the justice of their struggle, the moral weight of their cause, the generosity and strength of their commitment and their readiness to lay down their lives, and their closeness to the people, qualities which were more in evidence among the popular organisations than in other political groups. And he admired their values although he knew that there were non-believers as well as Christians in the popular organisations. This was no reason for him not to give the organisations his admiration and support. He was convinced that 'even beyond the boundaries of the church the power of Christ's redemption is actively at work, and the aspirations to liberation of individuals and groups, even though they do not call themselves Christians, are inspired by the Spirit of Jesus'

(Third Pastoral Letter, n 106).

Towards the end, though he kept up both his criticism as well as his support, he came to realise that the popular organisations had entered upon a stage which, in its context, he regarded positively. He had called for unity, and for the overcoming of sectarianism. With the creation of the Revolutionary Co-ordinating Committee of the Masses, and in the opening towards other democratic social and political forces, these ends seemed about to be attained. Archbishop Romero did not live to hear of the formation of the Democratic Front on 2 April, but he knew of the first steps that were being taken, and was delighted by them. In fact, through the archbishopric's Legal Aid Bureau he was in a way present in the 'Halt to the Repression' document signed by a number of democratic institutions. The formation of this Democratic Front was wanted by several democratic groups. But it was made possible by the openness of the Co-ordinating Committee and its desire to weld together other forces in society in support of the popular programme.

He was also pleased when the Co-ordinating Committee presented a unified platform, since that fact presupposed a wholly new form of unity. It was also a response to Archbishop Romero's explicit request that the people should know along which paths the Co-ordinating Committee wanted to lead the country. We cannot now know what he would have thought about the content of the platform. The only thing we have is his reply, given in the interview already quoted, when he was asked about it: 'I know of it, and I accept it as a basis for discussion among the people. There has to be a readiness to receive criticism and comment from every sector, so that it can be the people itself which creates the government it desires'.

Finally, in the last stage of the Co-ordinating Committee, one of his main concerns was that the new programme should respect the people's humane and religious values. The presence of many Christians in the popular organisations, and the readiness of the popular organisations and their Co-ordinating Committee to engage in dialogue with the church and other Christian institutions, appeared to him to give certain guarantees in that respect. He insisted so much on this partly because it was his clear duty as an archbishop in the church but also in part as a Salvadorean. The popular programme ought to find a place for Christianity, he argued, because Christianity was an important part of people's lives.

Archbishop Romero displayed great hopes of the popular programme while it was being drawn up, though without idealising it. He made suggestions for improving it, and was constantly demanding that it display greater maturity. From his homily of 20 January onwards he repeatedly referred to his hopes of it. Not that he *identified* himself with it, nor with any other current political programme because, as archbishop, he could not be identified with political programmes in the strict sense of the term. In any case he believed that it would be more fruitful for the development of the country if he kept a certain distance. But there is no doubt at all that, in the popular programme, he saw the best, and the most workable, translation into political terms of that option for the poor which he so radically defended in pastoral terms.

So it would be a mistake to present Archbishop Romero as a man of the 'centre', keeping himself equidistant from the 'left' and from the 'right'. It would be a mistake to imagine that Archbishop Romero acted on the *negative* principle of avoiding extremes. In fact he acted from *positive* principles, asking himself where there was more truth, greater justice, wider possibilities for peace. He found these values to a greater extent and with greater potential in the popular programme. He wanted to avoid the trap which the very terminology 'right', 'left' and 'centre' offers, as if it were the job of an archbishop to choose the 'centre' *ex officio*. In the interview quoted above he was asked what the 'left' meant for him. He replied, 'I don't call them the forces of the left but the forces of the people . . . What they call "the left" is the people. It is the organisation of the people . . . and their demands are the demands of the people'. Archbishop Romero did not choose not to choose — which, in effect, is what to be 'of the centre' means — but he opted for the people, he opted for the great mass of the poor which is the people.

3.3 The church's role in the present process

Archbishop Romero saw clearly that the country is passing through a process, a process involving conflict, in which the supporters of each of the three programmes are trying to push their own programme forward. He also saw clearly that it was the church's duty to pass judgement not only on the political programmes, but also on the process itself. The church should also insert itself into the process, as the church, in order to humanise it according to Christian values.

3.3.1 Archbishop Romero took a stand on the conflicts inherent in the process and, more specifically, on violence. His problem was to determine the legitimacy or illegitimacy of violence and — given that it is a fact — to humanise it as far as possible.
1. In making his fundamental ethical judgement on violence Archbishop Romero distinguished between initial violence and the violence of response. He recalled the traditional teaching on the proportionality of violence in legitimate defence and tried to distinguish between degrees of violence using the categories of Medellin.

Following Medellin, he firmly condemned the primary, initiating violence of institutional injustice which is translated into institutionalised violence and, in practice in El Salvador, into generalised repression. From this point of view he saw the violence of response as legitimate and just. He saw the setting up of the popular organisations as itself a first response to structural injustice and one whose methods were not inherently violent but based on social pressure. When these popular organisations, exercising their social pressure, are attacked, they have a legitimate right to defend themselves. This is how he put it in a carefully phrased paragraph in his fourth pastoral letter:

We are also aware that the great number of peasants, workers, slum dwellers and so on who have organised to defend their rights and to further legitimate changes in the structure of society, are simply regarded as 'terrorists' and 'subversives'. They are therefore arrested, tortured, they disappear, they are killed without any concern for the law or for those legal institutions which are there to protect them. They have no chance to defend themselves or to prove their innocence. Confronted by this unequal and unjust situation, they have frequently been forced to defend themselves, even to the point of having recourse to violence. And lately the response to this has been the arbitrary violence of the state.

Within the context of legitimate self-defence Archbishop Romero condemned what was out of proportion. He also condemned, though this was more typical of the para-military political groups than it was of the popular organisations, terrorist violence. Though at times it may be difficult to distinguish between armed violence which is legitimate and straightforward terrorism, Archbishop Romero took great care to analyse situations, and to condemn terrorism.

That is why it was not Archbishop Romero's habit to repeat the condemnation of violence 'wherever it comes from', but, in a manner that is rarely to be found in the language of bishops he said, 'The church cannot assert in a simplistic way that it condemns all forms of violence' (Fourth Pastoral Letter). He tried to analyse it carefully, and to judge each case on its merits.

2. But Archbishop Romero was not simply content to judge the legitimacy or otherwise of acts of violence. He also attempted to humanise those events which involved violence. Though there were cases when violence might be *just*, Archbishop Romero tried to make it *good* as well. He put people on their guard against those negative by-products of violence which can occur even when the violence is legitimate. He warned constantly about the need to overcome hate, to overcome the instinct for vengeance, the temptation to make violence the chief and the basic means of achieving one's ends. He vigorously condemned what he called the mysticism of violence.

More positively, he promoted the use of peaceful means and belief in their efficacy even when violence might be necessary to some extent. Archbishop Romero was not a pacifist pure and simple. By nature he was a peaceful man. As archbishop he was a pacifier in the strict sense of the word: he was a man who made peace. So as to humanise even the violence which was legitimate he repeatedly drew attention to all the other means necessary to the establishment of peace: justice, dialogue, truth, magnanimity.

3. Archbishop Romero was also aware of the possibility of armed insurrection. He dwelt on the subject in his last pastoral letter, and he often alluded to it in his final homilies. Conscious of the influence he had in society at large, he tried by his actions to prevent the growth of a war psychosis, though he had to

recognise that there were already so many dead that the situation resembled an undeclared civil war. But he was always trying to encourage people to avoid it, to find other means of bringing about radical changes in the country. So in the beginning he was moved to support the attempts of the first junta. Recent events raised in him the hope that the popular programme might gather so much impetus, and bring together so many different sectors in society, that change might be the most peaceful, and the least violent possible. Nonetheless he did not exclude the possibility of insurrection. He fought for reconciliation until the last, seeing that as one of his most important tasks. But when asked what would happen should reconciliation prove impossible, he replied laconically, 'It is a case of the insurrection which the church accepts when all peaceful means have been exhausted' (interview, 19 March 1980).

3.3.2 Archbishop Romero regarded the popular programme as the best *for* the Salvadoreans, the one most likely to guarantee lasting structures of justice. But his ecclesial sense made him insist constantly that this programme should draw on the best *of* the Salvadorean people and should also promote, once carried out, the values *of* Salvadoreans. In theological language, he was concerned about the *kingdom* of God and 'kingdom *people*'. It was in this deep sense, and not as a matter of routine, that he called for a conversion of structures and a conversion of hearts.

His interest in people and not just in structures was very evident, not only when he spoke as a Christian to Christians, but also when he spoke to the people of El Salvador as a whole. To Christians he emphasised the explicit values of Christianity, faith in God, prayer, openness to Christ, realities which, for him, as a Christian, really made people human. With others he put forward the purest Christian values, though they might not be recognised as Christian, as a contribution to the emergence of a new type of Salvadorean.

This new Salvadorean needed to be already in the making, in Archbishop Romero's view, as we have seen, even in conflict. These men and women needed to be thought of in terms of the future of a new society. Though we do not know what he thought of the manifesto of the Co-ordinating Committee, I believe that he would have insisted on analysing the human, cultural, spiritual and Christian values of Salvadoreans, and would have regarded this as the church's most typical contribution. He would have understood that this sort of document is customarily more concerned with an analysis of a country's structural problems, but he would have remarked that, although new structures no doubt help, they do not automatically resolve human problems. He would have recognised that structures are not changed merely by goodness of heart, but he would have recalled that neither will people's hearts change simply because of better structures. In this sense he used to stress that the popular programme ought to acknowledge, and enhance, all that is best in the people of El Salvador, in their cultural inheritance and religious values.

3.3.3 Archbishop Romero saw finally that to humanise this process the church must be present within it. It ought not simply to ignore it, or judge it merely from the outside, despite all the conflict and historical ambiguity which are inherent in any process. It is very clear that he himself was present within the process, both in his general activity as archbishop and in all those innumerable particular occasions when he took it upon himself to dialogue with, to mediate on behalf of, and to stand alongside the people. It is also clear that he wanted all Christians, including the clergy, to be involved in the process and not to try and escape from the most difficult aspect of it, that of associating themselves with politically committed Christians.

He believed that the church ought to be present in the process in a way which is specific to its nature. That is to say, the church ought to be an evangelical force which directly becomes a social force and indirectly a political one. He believed this ought to happen for the good of the process itself, and so that the church's support might be more effective. Although maintaining the specific character of the church's involvement in the process might seem less politically effective in the short term, Archbishop Romero was convinced, and history has borne him out, that in this way the church's influence would be greater and more humanising in the long term.

He did not believe that it was the church's proper role to direct the process. It was to make its presence felt in the manner of leaven. He did not regard it as *theoretically* the church's task

74

to undertake political leadership, though he himself gave immense social leadership. And *in practice* he knew that among the leaders in the process there were not only many Christians, but also unbelievers. The church should therefore be present, he argued, not through purely political mechanisms but rather through the objective weight of its truth, its arguments, its cogency, and its influence in society.

Archbishop Romero regarded the church's presence in the process as being of the highest importance both for the process itself and for the future of the church. A church which had not been present in the process might subsequently be displaced by those — *ex hypothesi* without the church — who had given their blood and their lives for the popular programme. He did not share the common belief that the church has an abstract right to have a voice and influence in society. A church which, for example, had abandoned the people in their process of change could not later claim to lead the people.

Finally, Archbishop Romero wanted the church to be present in the process for one simple, and profoundly Christian, reason: the incarnation. The first truth one says of Christ ought also be said of the church. Not infrequently, when the church is faced by new developments which involve conflict and ambiguity, it is tempted to stand on one side, to judge the developments from the outside. And not infrequently this attitude is defended by an appeal to the transcendence of the faith.

Archbishop Romero believed profoundly in the transcendence of the faith, of which the church is custodian, but he believed in it in a Christian manner. So he believed that the church ought to become incarnate in the world as it really is. It ought to maintain faith's transcendence not by alienating itself from, but by submerging itself in, particular situations, judging them, learning from them, always making them more human, always trying to eliminate what is dehumanising. The 'more' which constantly rises in an attempt to deepen the idea of humanity is what directs the church towards the authentic transformation of God. That is why, for this theological reason, Archbishop Romero believed that the church ought always to make itself present, and to do so in a manner which is proper to the church. If the church fails to be present in current developments, then it will simply stop being the Christian

75

church, the church of Jesus, the church which believes in God.

Let us end where we began. If Archbishop Romero played a leading role in the church and in society it was because of his profound faith in the God of Jesus. It was by being such a spiritual, such a religious man, such a follower of Jesus, not by ceasing to be one, but precisely by being one, that he was able to renew the life of the church and guide the country along the road of liberation.

His martyrdom has simply confirmed the truth of his life and his cause. His faith in God lead him to foresee his martyrdom. He looked upon it as the final service he could render to the church and to his country. In an interview with *Excelsior* of Mexico just two weeks before his death he put it like this:

I have frequently been threatened with death. I ought to say that, as a Christian, I do not believe in death without resurrection. If they kill me I will rise again in the people of El Salvador. I am not boasting, I say it with the greatest humility.

I am bound, as a pastor, by a divine command to give my life for those whom I love, and that is all Salvadoreans, even those who are going to kill me. If they manage to carry out their threats, from this moment I offer my blood for the redemption and resurrection of El Salvador.

Martyrdom is a grace from God which I do not believe I deserve. But if God accepts the sacrifice of my life, then may my blood be the seed of liberty, and a sign that hope will soon become a reality.

May my death, if it is accepted by God, be for the liberation of my people, and as a witness of hope in what is to come. Can you tell them, if they succeed in killing me, that I pardon and bless those who do it.

But I wish that they could realise that they are wasting their time. A bishop may die, but the church of God, which is the people, will never die.